Books : From Writer to Reader

DATE DUE

MAY 5 2000

inary power to change the life of an individual or

way of thinking of an entire society.

ks play a vital part in our lives. When young we are

ed to the world of fantasy and beauty by them, not

means of words but also through colorful illustrations.

chools, w   eans of them, and as we

their ra   oader. Books are essential

nt to stu   or engineering—or really

47
TOLIVER'S SECRET   —6841—

Whenever she passed a dark shadow of a farmhouse sitting behind a stone wall, she could smell the smoke from the chimney. There must be people inside. People eating bowls of piping hot stew, sitting beside a crackling fire. Perhaps children were pulling on nightshirts that had been warmed at the fire. Perhaps they were climbing into bed and putting their feet against warm bricks wrapped in wool. Mother had always warmed her bed for her this way at home.

Not a crack of light showed at the windows. Although a dog barked at the sound of her feet crunching in the snow, the doors remained shut.

And then, far ahead, she saw a light no bigger than a needle prick in the dark.

"Maybe it's Mr. Shannon's tavern!" she cried, and tried to run. But her cold wet feet would not obey her. They stumbled and slid on the frozen road and she could not make them hurry.

As she slipped from one uneven hoof mark to the next, she found herself saying over and over, "I shall run and not faint: I shall walk and not grow weary." Somehow, the words made her think of Grandfather. She remembered him sitting by the fire in the kitchen with his little reading glasses on his nose and the old Dutch Psalm Book in his hands. "They that wait upon the Lord," she could hear her grandfather's cheerful voice, "they shall walk and not be weary: they shall run and not faint." It made her feel better to think of the words that Grandfather read aloud and believed so firmly.

When at last she came close to the light she saw that it poured from an open doorway. She knew it was the doorway of a blacksmith's shop by the clang of a hammer on an iron anvil. Wearily she stumbled up to the door and leaned against the doorframe. When she could catch her breath she would ask the smith the way to the Jolly Fox Tavern.

The small barn was filled with dark shadows and flickering lights, for at one side the fire in the fireplace glowed on a hearth that was almost as high as a table. How good it was to feel the warm air blow over her as she stepped inside.

The blacksmith was startled when he looked up from the anvil where he was beating a horseshoe into shape. His eyes shown bright in his grimy face.

"What brings you here, boy?" he said sharply. "It's a cold night to be out."

"Oh, sir, I'm frozen into an icicle."

"Step up to the fire, then, but don't alarm the horse."

With the barn brightened by the fire, Ellen could see at the other side of the room an old gray horse waiting to be shod. And in the corner beside the horse a big man sitting on a barrel. He was wearing a plaid

BOOKS

From Writer to Reader

HOWARD GREENFELD

Crown Publishers, Inc., New York

Also by Howard Greenfeld

They Came to Paris
F. Scott Fitzgerald
Gertrude Stein : A Biography

The text of this book is set in 12 pt. Trump.
The illustrations are line, black and white halftone, and full color.

Library of Congress Cataloging in Publication Data
Greenfeld, Howard.
    Books:from writer to reader.
    Summary: Follows a book through the various stages
of publishing, printing and marketing.
    1. Books—Juvenile literature. 2. Book industries
and trade—Juvenile literature. [1. Books. 2. Book
industries and trade. 3. Printing] I. Title.
Z116.A2G74   1976   808'.02   76-15991
ISBN 0-517-52620-4 Hardbound
ISBN 0-517-53493-2 Paperback

Acknowledgments

This book is the result of many years' experience in book publishing. Nonetheless, I could not have written it without the help of several people who gave generously of their time and knowledge as I was writing it. Among those I would like to thank are Alice and Bob Cromie, Barbara Bannon, Philip Spitzer, Beth Greenfeld, Belle Becker Sideman, Barbara G. Hennessy, Milt Wackerow, and Freda Barry Brown.

For assistance in gathering illustrations and for granting permission to reproduce them, I would like to thank the following: American Book-Stratford Press, The American Library Association, *The Booklist*, R.R. Bowker Company, Esther Wood Brady, *Bulletin of the Center for Children's Books*, Crown Publishers, Inc., Richard Cuffari, Diane de Groat, Halliday Lithograph Corporation, Harris Corporation, *The Horn Book*, Tamara Hovey, Houghton Mifflin Company, IBM, International Paper, *Kirkus Reviews*, Lingen Verlag Köln, Linda T. Mead, The Mergenthaler Linotype Company, Walter Miles, Louis Monaco, Jr., Hester Mundis, *Philadelphia Inquirer*, Clarkson N. Potter, Inc., *Publishers Weekly*, Royal

Composing Room, *School Library Journal*, Society of Authors' Representatives, Robert M. Schwartz, J-C Suarès, The University of Chicago Press, Vandersons Corporation, Pat Voehl, John Wallner, Paula Winter.

Very special thanks are due Norma Jean Sawicki, without whom this book about books would not have become a book.

Introduction

They entertain us or inform us; they make us laugh or make us cry; they please us, or they anger us. They have the extraordinary power to change the life of an individual or even the way of thinking of an entire society.

Books play a vital part in our lives. When young we are introduced to the world of fantasy and beauty by them, not only by means of words but also through illustrations. In our schools, we are educated by means of them, and, as we grow up, their range becomes even broader. Books are essential if we want to study law or medicine or engineering—or really anything at all. From them, too, we can learn to cook a meal or sew a dress or play chess.

Television programs and movies are fine; they also entertain and inform. But with a book we can stop where we like, think it over and go on, or we can reread those passages which stimulate or entertain us the most, as well as the ones that might have puzzled us the first time around. We can put them on a shelf, too, and come back to them another day.

Books are indeed such a fundamental part of our lives—it is impossible to imagine a world without them—that many people take them for granted. They somehow appear, almost miraculously; we have them and read them and enjoy them....

I have spent many years in the world of books. I have written them and edited them and published them and sold them. Throughout these years, many people—those who do not take books for granted—have asked me questions. How do you write a book? What do you do with a manuscript once you've written it? What does an editor do? How is a book designed? How is it printed, and how is it bound?

This small book is an attempt to answer these and other questions, and by means of these answers it will become clear that the process of conceiving and making a book is a long, complicated, and difficult one. Books don't just grow. They are the result of teamwork, of many creative people joining together to produce a work that each hopes may, in some small way, enrich the world. It's not all idealism, of course. There are strictly commercial and business considerations involved; book publishing is, after all, a business and must be conducted as such. Yet there is something special in it, an indefinable excitement in the knowledge that each book will have a life of its own, will survive longer than other essential products—like shoes or cars or dresses—in someone's home, in a public library, or in the mind of the reader.

Howard Greenfeld
Pieve di Camaiore, Italy

The Writer

The book inevitably begins with the writer, without whom there could be no book. His or her job is to fill blank pieces of paper with words and sentences—the right words in the right order to convey ideas or thoughts or facts or visions or dreams to a prospective reader. No one writer is like another; they are individuals, writing for different reasons with different goals in mind. Each writer has different working habits. Some work mornings, some work afternoons, and some work at night. There are writers who can create for eight hours a day and some who can work no more than two hours a day. There are no regular routines, as in an office, and it is impossible to order a writer to work a certain number of hours per day or per week and expect that author to obey. Creation, the act of writing a book, depends on many things: on mood, on inspiration, even on the weather.

The method and place of creation, too, differ from writer to writer. Some writers must use a typewriter, while others prefer writing in longhand. Even in the latter case, there are differences, since some prefer a pen and some a pencil. Some writers need the silence of the country; some need the noise and excitement of a city. Some will write the whole book before revising and polishing the manuscript, while others prefer to work slowly and perfect each passage as they go along. There are even cases of writers who like to write standing up, though it is undoubtedly true that most prefer to do their work while sitting down.

So we see that writers differ among themselves in very many ways. A writer is not a machine, but an individual creator. His job is a difficult and often a lonely one, and when he begins his work, he cannot predict just how much he will accomplish; some days he can write ten pages with ease, and other days he is hardly able to write more than ten sentences.

The form in which a writer chooses to express himself varies, too. There are men and women who write poetry or children's books or plays, works of fiction or works of nonfiction, though of course it is not necessary for any one author to restrict himself to any single genre. Many novelists have also written plays, just as many biographers have written children's books, although each of these does require a specialized skill.

A poet is most concerned with language, with the sound and rhythm of words as well as their precise meanings. A playwright is, of course, concerned with dialogue and with dramatic movement, the playwright's work generally being destined for performance on a stage by actors, before an audience. In general, however, books fall into two categories, fiction and nonfiction.

Works of fiction are works of the imagination, the most common being the novel or the short story, while nonfiction includes all works of fact: biography, history, science, philosophy, and so on. For a novelist—or short story writer—there are few limitations. He or she is free to create characters of his or her own choosing, settings both real and imaginary, stories both logical and illogical. These writers can write realistic books about things and people that might be familiar to all of us, or they might create in works of fantasy the most bizarre or unfamiliar characters and situations, totally unfamiliar to us.

These authors usually begin with a character or set of characters. Very often the writer will have no plot when he begins to write—merely a set of characters who especially interest him or her, and by placing these diverse characters in certain situations, a plot may evolve. From these characters then, a story will grow. All peoples, from all times, have been interested in tales about people, in stories, in the suspense that many stories involve. A formula of universal interest might well be: How will he or she or they—obviously, they must all be people of interest—solve a given problem? The problem could well be a murder, or finding a way of life, or a complex romantic situation, but, whatever it is, it will be of interest if the persons concerned are of interest.

Some novelists carefully plan their stories before beginning the long job of writing them. They outline chapter by chapter; they make brief sketches of the characters for their own use; they make physical plans of a house or a town that may serve as the setting for their story.

Other novelists are actually led by their characters, having no idea of where these characters may lead them by the time the story is completed. In a way, they create the characters who in turn create the plot.

However one works, the novelist must become deeply involved in the lives of the characters of his or her novel. This involvement does not end during "off" hours: his creations are inevitably with him twenty-four hours a day. They become an integral part of his or her life as long as the story is being written, and this involvement/identification begins well before the actual words are put onto paper and lasts well beyond the point at which the actual writing is finished.

A novelist or short story writer writes, above all, out of a need to write, a desire to describe the people or places, or a will to tell a given story. The writer conveys a mood, brings to life his characters, creates an atmosphere of time or place, real or unreal. The successful novel involves the reader in a world other than his own, or illuminates for him parts of his own world that he

```
                    Summary of Chapter 1X

          On Tuesday morning Marcy woke up with another bad dream She had

     been in a deep well and she couldn't get out because that toad was at the top

     of the well and he kept grinning down at her.

          Toby kept marching all over the house,beating his wooden drum,

     until Mama made him stay out of doors."I am going to war," he cried.I am

     going to be a drummer boy."

          Marcy wanted to start for Pierce's Mill immediately.It

     would be fun to live in an old mill with aany other families.They would

     cook out of doors and wade in the mill-pond.It would be cool out there

     in the woods along Rock Creek.Marcy kept begging Mama to leave.

          But Mama was undecided.She said she was going to call on

     Aunt Dolley and ask her opinion.Mama called the president's wife Aunt Dolley

     because she had known her ever since she was a small girl in Philadelphia.

     Of course she called her Mrs.Madison when she spoke to her--since she

     was the First Lady of the land.

          Mama took the children with her.They walked because there were

     no carriages to rent as Mama would have done at any other time.

          At the front door of the big white house,Mama said"Now children

     remember your manners.Why where is Toby?"

          Toby was missing.


          (Descrition of President's house and of Dolley Madison)


          There were two other callers,but they had come without their

     children. Mrs.Livingston and Mrs.Ward had grown up in Philadephia,too.
```

*Author's chapter sum-
mary from a work in prog-
ress*

has never examined. His tools for this are language;
words serve him just as colors and forms serve a painter
and notes and sounds serve a musician.

There are schools for novelists, courses in writing the novel or the short story, and these may have their uses. But no academic training can make a man or woman into a successful writer of fiction. A novelist or short story writer depends on his or her own experience and imagination, on sensitivity and the power of observation. In addition, of course, there *must* be a love of and a feeling for words, for the proper language with which to express these experiences and insights into human beings. A novelist creates a world and the people in it and the situations that these people may find themselves in; there are few, if any, lessons he or she can learn from study, other than the reading of other books and the knowledge of how other authors may or may not have solved their problems.

Such is not the case with the writer of nonfiction—that is, biography, history, science, all works that are dependent not on the imagination but on fact. The writer of such works must be knowledgeable about the field in which he or she chooses to write, and academic training will be helpful in many cases and absolutely essential in others.

Any biographer or historian or writer on science will be required to spend many months or often years researching his subject. This means an enormous amount of reading, of poring through books in libraries, of tracing facts to their original sources. While doing the research, every writer of nonfiction learns what every reader should know—that not everything found in books is necessarily true. A researcher finds what seems an often incredible number of discrepancies between one source and another. Because one book will give one date and one another—and often a third one can be found in a third book—the writer of nonfiction must do his best to go back to the original source, to find out the truth.

In addition to reading everything possible about his subject, the writer will often find it necessary to interview various people connected with his subject. This would include other authorities in the field, eyewitnesses to an event, or friends or acquaintances of the subject of a biography.

In the course of all this work that takes place prior to the actual writing of the book, the writer will be taking voluminous notes. He will distinguish his sources and choose which authorities to believe and which to doubt. He must then be selective, above all keeping in mind the audience for whom he is writing. Obviously, a work meant for scholars will require more detail than one meant for the general reader, just as a book written for children will have to be approached differently from one written for adults.

With his facts gathered and his reader in mind, the writer then must organize his book—in the most readable, dramatic, as well as logical sequence. If the gathering and selection of factual material require scholarship and intelligence, the interpretation and organization of this material require imagination and literary skill. Many an interesting subject has been made dull by his

Had been newspaper reporter in US and correspondent abroad.

Jolas — Born in US of Lorraine parents, spent childhood in L.
1844   New Jersey   French father - German mother
and returned to US at 15. Fluent in English, French + German. Senator
and wrote poetry in

About 33 when 1st t published.
(Seraphson) "a very lovable man" In spite of Josephson's
opposition to JS, J appointed him contributing editor of t

Poverty in US, first made living as grocery boy in Brooklyn, reporter in
Waterbury, conn during Palmer raids   BOYLE-266

Salon in 1927-8 became a "chapel for the idolaters of J. S." (Josephson

Physical — broad-shouldered, heavy-set, fine head, wild poetic gaze
Short, dark, shiny-faced, full of verve

Maria Jolas — MacDonald Tall, good-looking, from Kentucky, Statuesque, handsome
warm, hospitable, musical, sensitive, full of enthusiasm for all forms of mod. art
Donated much money to Joyce + family when he was going blind.

Jolases (Crosby) "Grand, gifted people, with minds like
new brooms, hearts like hearts."

Author's working notes for a biography

biographer, while many less interesting figures have been made more exciting by their more gifted biographers, just as a historical event of minor importance can be made fascinating by an imaginative author.

In the end, fiction and nonfiction alike are the result of a writer's inspiration and/or interest, but it is essential to remember the writer's dedication as well. It is popular to think of a writer's life as being glamorous and romantic; however, the opposite is generally true. There is creative satisfaction involved in the writing of a book—just as there is in all creative fields—but more than that there is hard work, and every writer spends far more time writing than he does at well-publicized cocktail parties. Financial sacrifice, too, is usually involved, as few writers are able to earn very much money for their work. In fact, the large majority of writers have full-time jobs to support themselves and their families and must write at night or during weekends.

But the true writer writes—out of a need to express himself or herself or to inform or educate the public. It is this passion, and it is no less than that, that drives most writers to undertake the difficult task of writing a book.

He or she hopes that his words will be set into type and then printed and bound, and the result—a book—will be then sold to the reader. The benefit, whether it be pleasure or insight or knowledge, that this reader will receive from the book will make the struggle that goes into writing it ultimately worthwhile to its author.

The Literary Agent

After a great deal of work, long periods of hope, and often longer periods of despair, the writer has finished writing the book. He or she should know that it must be neatly typed, double-spaced. It is at this point that many new writers feel helpless: it's obviously not enough to write the book—it must be read. And the words set down on manuscript paper by the writer cannot be read by a number of people until they are put into the form of a book and thus made suitable for reading. A publisher and only a publisher will do this.

But there are many publishers, and it is necessary to find the right one. A few writers may know someone in publishing and eagerly submit their manuscripts to their friends or acquaintances. Others may know of an invaluable guide to publishing houses called *Literary Market Place* and select a potential publisher from among the many listed there. Still others could be

"Its Goose Creek."

"I said its called Tiber Creek now."

Eben snorted."Goose Creek *is* a better name--for a country town."

That made Marcy angry."Why,this is the capital of the United

States of America."

"Humph," said Eben."Some capital. Cow pastures right next to

the main street.Chickens running loose. Philadelphia was a better capital."

Marcie had to admit to herself that chickens and pigs and ducks

on Pennsylvania Avenue did make Washington look like a country town.

Eben sneered."In Philadelphia the streets are paved. And there

are steeet lights."

"Wahington is going to be a great city someday--when its

finished.

"Humph,"said Eben again."A great city right in the middle

of the wilderness. Inthe river at Philadelphia there are ships from

all over the world."

" Oh,Philadelphia--Philadelphia--Philadelphia!" snapped Marcy."Why

don't you just go back to Philadelphia?''

Eben's face grew white with anger.He narrowed his eyes as he

looked at her.Marcy was frighted by the fury she saw there.

At last he said in a voice that was almost strangled."You

know well enough I can't go back."

Suddenly he raised his arm and slapped her across the face

with the dead fish.

An unedited manuscript page

among those very few readers who pay attention to the name of a publishing house whose books seem to be similar to the ones they have written and so they send their manuscripts off to these houses.

Any of these methods may help, but at this stage the writer may want professional help, and one way he can obtain that help is from a literary agent.

A literary agent is a scout for talented writers and often a helpful and perceptive editor; the agent, too, is a businessman or a businesswoman whose success or failure in handling the affairs of a client will determine the success or failure of the literary agency. The agent is often in the best position to know not only what is salable and what is not, but also exactly what publisher would be best suited to publish a particular work. There are all kinds of agencies—large ones with staffs of fifty, and small ones with a staff of one. Nonetheless, it is always one agent who is responsible for the work of each author—whether that agent operates alone or as part of a large organization—and each agent has his or her special tastes and qualifications. The agent must, above all, be in touch with publishers, must know what is being published by each house and just what the taste of each editor at each house is likely to be. The agent must always be on the lookout for talent, recognize the potentialities of young, unknown authors, and be willing to encourage and promote an author or that author's work through guidance and constructive suggestions. The good agent is selective, knowing that his or her business will suffer if inferior works are offered to a publisher, just as he or she must be willing and able to advise the author as to ways in which a manuscript could be improved, if that manuscript shows promise. In many ways, a good agent acts as a clearinghouse for a publisher—eliminating the hopelessly bad and encouraging the good. It is for this reason that a manuscript submitted by a careful agent, known for his or her good taste and knowledge of the market, may often receive more careful attention than will a manuscript submitted by either an unknown author or an irresponsible agent.

Many writers, who feel they can use the services of an agent in marketing a manuscript, are—with good reason—puzzled as to how to find this agent. There are, however, various ways of finding a list of reputable, well-established agents: through *Literary Market Place*, through The Authors Guild, which is an association of writers, or by consulting a list provided by an organization called the Society of Authors' Representatives. With any one of these lists on hand, the author should choose and write to one or even several agents, describing the work he wishes to submit, giving a resume of his or her background and experience, and, of course, mentioning any previously published work. No manuscript should ever be submitted to an agent before that agent requests it; many agencies are unwilling or unable to take on new clients, and sending the manuscript itself before it has been requested is a waste of both

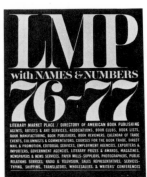

Literary Market Place

From a brochure published by the Society of Author's Representatives

How To Find An Agent

The author, before sending his manuscript, should write a short letter describing his work and giving a brief resume of his interests. If his work has previously been published or performed, he should so inform the agent. An author may query several agents at the same time; however, he should submit his manuscript for reading to only one agent at a time. For the best possible consideration, an author should send an agent the original typed copy plus return postage. The author should always retain a carbon or machine copy.

Any of the following will supply a list of reputable agents:

1. The Authors Guild, 234 West 44 Street, New York, N. Y. 10036, to its members.

2. Nationally known book publishers.

3. National magazines.

In 1928, a group of literary and play agents organized the Society of Authors' Representatives, Inc. (101 Park Avenue, New York, N. Y. 10017). This is a voluntary association of agents, whose individual members subscribe to the ethical practices described herein. The SAR regrets that it cannot recommend *individual* member agents. Authors are advised to write directly to agents in the appropriate category (L or D) in the manner described above, if they wish to contact an SAR agent about their work. The following is a list of the membership of the association.

Cyrilly Abels
119 West 57 Street
New York, N. Y. 10019
(L)

American Play Company, Inc.
52 Vanderbilt Avenue
New York, N. Y. 10017
(D)

Julian Bach Literary Agency, Inc.
3 East 48 Street
New York, N. Y. 10017
(L)

Bill Berger Associates, Inc.
535 East 72 Street
New York, N. Y. 10021
(L)

Lurton Blassingame
60 East 42 Street
New York, N. Y. 10017
(L)

Georges Borchardt, Inc.
145 East 52 Street
New York, N. Y. 10022
(L)

Brandt & Brandt
101 Park Avenue
New York, N. Y. 10017
(L)

Curtis Brown, Ltd.
60 East 56 Street
New York, N. Y. 10022
(L-D)

James Brown Associates, Inc.
22 East 60 Street
New York, N. Y. 10022
(L-D)

Knox Burger Associates, Ltd.
39½ Washington Square South
New York, N. Y. 10012
(L)

John Cushman Associates, Inc.
25 West 43 Street
New York, N. Y. 10036
(L)

Joan Daves
515 Madison Avenue
New York, N. Y. 10022
(L)

Ann Elmo Agency, Inc.
52 Vanderbilt Avenue
New York, N. Y. 10017
(L-D)

Harold Freedman Brandt & Brandt
    Dramatic Department, Inc.
101 Park Avenue
New York, N. Y. 10017
(D)

Samuel French, Inc.
25 West 45 Street
New York, N. Y. 10036
(D)

time and money. In any case, though an author might write a letter of inquiry to several agents at once, he or she should never submit a work to more than one agent at a time.

Once the agent has shown interest in a work, he or she will, in most cases, read that work without charging the author a fee. There are some agents, however, who do charge a reading fee for each manuscript submitted and others who charge what they call an "editorial fee." The former might be justified on the grounds that an agent spends a large amount of time reading works that might never be salable and should be paid for that time. The editorial fee, however, for which an agent promises to edit a manuscript so that it might be suitable for submission to a publisher, is not justifiable. The author's manuscript should be edited by the editor at the publishing house that undertakes to publish it and not by an agent—though there is no harm and sometimes benefit from an agent's suggestions once that agent has agreed to handle the manuscript. This, however, is part of the agent's job, one for which there should be no charge. A writer must realize that, just as there are good and bad writers, there are also good and bad agents.

Once the writer has found an agent who is sympathetic to his work and understands what he is trying to do, the relationship between these two can be very close. It is, of course, best that the writer understands just what can and cannot be expected of the agent.

The agent reads and evaluates the manuscript on hand, and on the basis of this evaluation submits the manuscript to the publisher who in his judgment is best suited to publish it. Editors move from house to house, and the agent must keep up to date with these changes and with the special taste of each editor; he must know which editor would be most sympathetic to the work of any given writer—and to that writer's personality. Markets, too, change, and an agent should be aware of these changes, of trends, and of fashions. Once the manuscript has been accepted for publication, the agent must perform the complicated task of negotiating the contract (this will be discussed later). As part of this contract, however, the agent will most probably take on certain responsibilities himself by retaining specified rights on behalf of the author and trying to sell them himself. These rights include dramatic rights—for radio, the net price received shall be less than the manufacturing costs, no royalties shall be payable.

(h) ~~% of the royalties received by the Publisher from a foreign publisher where~~ such foreign publisher pays a royalty on sheets, separate from the Publisher's ~~charges~~ for the sheets;

(i) _____ % of the sums received by the Publisher from the disposition of rights granted to it under paragraph 1 (b) hereof (publication in the [British] Commonwealth of Nations exclusive of Canada);

(j) _____ % of the sums received by the Publisher from the disposition of rights ~~granted to it under paragraph 1 (x) hereof (translation rights);~~

10 (a) The Publisher shall have exclusive control and the exclusive right in behalf of both parties hereto to dispose of the following publishing and mechanical and other recording rights in the Work ~~throughout the world and in all languages~~ reprint, whether hard- or soft-cover edition (including sets and omnibus volumes), selection, digest, abridgment, condensation, second serialization, ~~syndication~~ book club, ~~microfilming recording~~ ~~computer storage~~ syndication, Braille, ~~reading (direct or communicated) of the text of the~~ Work, ~~comic-strip and three-dimensional reproduction of characters.~~ Upon disposition of any of the foregoing rights, the net proceeds thereof shall be divided equally between the Author and the Publisher. ~~Upon other exploitation by the Publisher of the mechanical recording rights to be distributed in a tape or record form, the Publisher shall pay to the Author 10% of the net proceeds received by the Publisher as a result thereof~~

(b) ~~The Publisher shall have the exclusive control of and the exclusive right in be-~~ half of both parties hereto to dispose of dramatic, dramatico-musical, motion picture, public reading and other non-dramatic performing, radio and/or television rights in the Work throughout the world and in all languages, and the proceeds of such disposition shall be divided _____ % to the Author and _____ % to the Publisher; all contracts relating to these rights shall be subject to the approval of the Author, which approval shall not be unreasonably withheld.

(c) The Publisher shall have the exclusive control and the exclusive right in behalf of both parties hereto to dispose of first serialization of the Work in full length, condensed or abridged versions in one part before publication, and the net proceeds of each disposition ~~shall be 75% to the Author and 25% to the Publisher.~~

(d) The Author further agrees that in the event of an infringement by another party in the rights granted to the Publisher or rights of exclusive grant by the Publisher, the Publisher may at his option participate in the action brought by the Author against the infringing party to recover damages resulting from the infringement, and the net recovery shall be

In the territories stipulated in paragraph 1a

In the event of any major reprint or book club sale, the Publisher shall seek the agent's consent; such consent shall not be unreasonably withheld.

Subsidiary rights held by an agent are crossed out in the publisher's contract

television, motion picture, or theatrical adaptation; first serial rights—that is, rights to print parts, or even the whole, of a book in a magazine before the book is actually published; and, because most agents have representatives or affiliates in foreign countries, rights to publish the book either in another language or in Great Britain. Disposing of these rights can involve a great deal of work, but it can be most profitable for the agent.

The agent collects all the money—whether from the publishing house or other sources—that the author earns from the book and passes it on to him or her, after deducting the agent's commission, which is almost always 10 percent of the total amount earned by the au-

ROYALTY STATEMENT
For the period 3/1/75   through 8/31/75

AUTHOR: PAYABLE TO:
TITLE:

RETAIL PRICE: $4.50
_____

REGULAR TRADE SALES:

6,501	copies sold at a royalty of	5% of	4.50	$ 1,462.73
	copies sold at a royalty of	% of		
	copies sold at a royalty of	% of		

RETAIL SALES:

| | copies sold at a royalty of | % of | | |

SPECIAL and FOREIGN SALES:

1,100	copies sold at a royalty of	5% of	2.25	123.75
311	copies sold at a royalty of	2½% of	4.50	34.99
50	copies sold at a royalty of	5% of	1.80	4.50
200	copies sold at a royalty of	5% of	2.43	24.30

TOTAL ROYALTIES: $ 1,650.27

OTHER INCOME:
  Book Club Rights   **Weekly Reader**   3/24/75 $ 1,625.00
  Reprint Rights
  British Empire Income
  Translation Rights
  Permissions Granted

        TOTAL OTHER INCOME:
        TOTAL ROYALTIES and OTHER INCOME: $ 3,275.27

DEDUCTIONS:
  Advance Royalty $
  Sundry Charges
  Book Purchases
  Unearned Balance From Previous Statement

        TOTAL DEDUCTIONS:
        TOTAL EARNINGS DUE: $ 3,275.27

A royalty statement in which the author's advance has already been earned thor, for as long as the work brings in money—even if the author and agent have in the meantime separated. The agent, too, examines royalty statements, often requesting corrections, and the agent often checks on the publisher's handling of the book in its various stages of publication as well as after that.

The agent must know realistically what to expect both as an advance, which will be paid to the author against future royalty, and as a royalty; asking for too large an advance or too high a royalty percentage might well lose a sale. This is part of the good business sense essential in an agent, for he or she represents the author in all of the latter's business dealings with the publisher.

There are limitations, however, to what an agent can or should do. He or she simply cannot sell an unsalable work—no agent can be expected to perform a miracle. An agent, though helpful editorially at times, is not an editor and thus cannot be expected to edit a manuscript or teach a writer how to write. Nor can an agent be asked to spend too much time on any single client. An author, deeply involved in his or her own work, may mistakenly believe that he or she is the agent's only—or at least most important—client. This is obviously not the case, and just as an agent must understand the author's needs, that author must understand the agent's limitations. With both parties keeping that in mind, their relationship can be a rewarding and mutually beneficial one.

The Publishing House

With the help of a literary agent, or without it, the manuscript's next destination is a publishing house. There the decision to publish, or not to publish, will be made; and if that decision is a positive one, it is the responsibility of the publishing house to bring the work to the public. For this reason, it is most helpful for the author to have some idea of the structure of that hard-to-define organization and its workings.

A publishing house is made up of a group of variously creative people working together to produce and make available to the public a book—each book being a different and unique product that will be both valuable artistically and profitable commercially. These two goals are of equal importance, and, though they sometimes come into conflict, neither can be forgotten in the long and complicated process of publishing a book.

No two publishing houses are the same, and each acquires, through the list of books it publishes, a special character. They differ in size, too—there are small houses that have a staff of three people, and there are large houses with hundreds of people. Basically, however, they must all perform the same functions and are thus divided into similar departments.

The publisher himself, often the owner of the company, is the overall director, whose spirit and interests should guide the policy of the house and who coordinates the work of the various departments of the house. He or she is the person ultimately responsible for the books selected and for the manner in which they are published. There are basically two kinds of publishers. One might be called the "corporate" publisher, whose chief concern is business and efficiency, while the other is the "personal" publisher, a person whose individual taste is strongly reflected in the nature of the books presented to the public and is somewhat more concerned with artistic values than with business (though profit and loss are as much part of his publishing house as they are of the "corporate" publisher's). The "personal" publisher, in any case, is ideally a person whose courage and vision bring to the reader works of daring and originality—works often ahead of their time—and in the past these publishers have made major contributions to American literature. Today, more and more small houses are being bought by huge corporations, many (but not all) concerned far less with literature than with profit, but just as some small, good houses are absorbed,

Houghton Mifflin Company Boston

Clarkson N. Potter, Inc./Publisher
NEW YORK

Two publishers' imprints and colophons

other small, personal publishers are taking their places. These latter need both courage and money to found what is inevitably a very difficult business, one that is slow to build. However, no matter how great the risks, new publishers will be born as long as there are men and women devoted to the beauty and power of the written word. This is not to say that the large publisher cannot be a positive and valuable force in American publishing, but it is to be hoped that both large and small publishers continue to survive and prosper.

No publisher, no matter how large or small, or how gifted, can work alone, and he is inevitably dependent on those men and women who work with him in the various departments of the publishing house. These departments are, generally, the following: the editorial department; art, design, and production; publicity, sales, promotion, and advertising. The first two are concerned largely with the making of the book, its preparation and manufacture. The other departments mentioned are concerned largely with doing everything possible to see that any given book is promoted, and sold, to the largest possible public.

In addition, of course, there is the business department, which is concerned with paying bills for work done and making and collecting invoices for books sold; as well as the shipping department, which must see that books reach their destination.

All of these many parts of a publishing house work together and cooperate through the many stages that lead to the publication of a book. They frequently consult and advise each other, and all of their efforts should be carefully coordinated. For this reason, it is obviously useful that members of each department have at least some knowledge of the work done in other departments. An editor with a knowledge of the problems of book production is far more valuable than an editor who knows nothing about the actual manufacturing of a book. By the same token, the production department should be aware of the problems facing the sales department, just as the publicity department must keep in contact with the editorial department....

Obviously, a publishing house draws upon a large variety of creative skills—literary, artistic, technical, promotional, and commercial. All of these must come together as each book is the result of a common effort of several people, each of whom has a different talent and skill. As with any group of people working together, there are bound to be differences of opinion, honest differences of judgment as to what method would bring about the best result. These disagreements concern what books are to be published, how much is to be spent on their manufacture, what ways they might best be publicized and, finally, sold. These differences, however, far from harming a book or its sales, should really improve them by stimulating all efforts toward turning out the best possible book in the most economically sound way.

The Decision to Publish

The first important decision to be made in a publishing house is to select from the large number of manuscripts submitted those that will be accepted for publication. It is most often a very difficult decision, and very many factors are involved in making it.

Book publishing is a uniquely complex field, the publisher often being torn between his obligation to publish works of literary merit and the necessity to sell enough copies of any given book to make enough money to continue to publish more books. Publishing is a business and must be run as a business in order to survive. Publishers must show a financial profit just as any business must. On the other hand, it differs from most businesses in that the publisher has a moral duty to see that works of artistic or educational value—even those that have but a small chance of being commercially successful—are made available to the public. The publishers of the early work of some of the greatest writers of our time—Joyce and Faulkner, for example—knew that these books would not be financially profitable, yet they published them.

The decision whether or not to publish a book is made in many different ways, depending on the size of the publishing house, its economic structure, the nature of its list, and the makeup of its staff.

A single enthusiastic editor or publisher may be so carried away by a manuscript that he or she will fight to see that the work is accepted. In other cases, an editorial board, consisting of several editors, each of whom has read the manuscript, might discuss the pros and cons at an editorial meeting and then reach a decision. In still other cases, the manuscript might be submitted to the sales department, and the opinion of the salesmen as to the book's commercial value might be the decisive factor.

Fiction and nonfiction will be judged in different ways. A novel, a play, poetry, or a collection of short stories is more likely to be accepted on the basis of the work's literary merit and the publisher's feelings about the author's potential to write more books in the future. Often an editor might say that, though a first novel is flawed, the author shows such superior talent that his or her book is worth publishing in order to encourage that author to go on to write more books—for the same publisher, of course. In a business sense, that author becomes an investment for the future. Indeed, many writ-

```
(Please include synopsis, critique, and any information concerning author).
```

```
This story is about a ten-year-old girl who is allowed to
indulge many small fears until her grandfather asks her to
dress up as a boy and carry a message across enemy lines
to General Washington.  The message is hidden inside a snuff-
box, and baked in a loaf of bread. The adventure is strong,
and that is what keeps the reader interested.  The characters
are not alive enough, and certain scenes are not well-enough
thought out to give the story real integrity.  The change
from scared Sara to brave girl-dressed-up-as boy is accom-
plished too quickly, and there are scenes where other
characters do not behave realistically in terms of the action the
author has established.  Although it definitely needs revision,
there is sufficiently strong material here to make the direction
for change rather clear.  The style is easy, light and
graceful.
```

```
It would be useful to know whether this is based on a true story,
and to what extent the author has authenticated the details
of the period.
```

A reader's report

```
I'd be glad to write her.
```

ers whose first novels have failed commercially have gone on to become best-selling, or at least commercially successful, authors in later years.

When it comes to the decision regarding a work of nonfiction, the publisher has at his disposal certain facts that will make his decision an easier one. For example, a travel book on Italy might be submitted to a publisher who examines it and finds it both well written and informative. That's not enough. The publisher must find out how many books about Italy have been published, how many are still in print—that is, available to the public—how well they have sold or are selling, just how the manuscript he is considering differs from these other books, how much knowledge and information the manuscript in question adds to those already published. In other words, he must determine how much interest there is in the subject and must ask himself why a reader would buy his book rather than any of the other books available.

These decisions cannot be made too quickly. In back of each publisher's mind there must always be those two questions of artistic and financial responsibility. The decision to publish a book is a commitment of much money, time, and effort. Because of this, before offering a contract to an author, it is often essential to have at least a rough idea of just how a book will be manufactured and how much it will cost. The more information the publisher has, the easier it will be for him to come to a decision; the facts determined in advance can also serve as the basis for the terms of an eventual contract.

For each projected book, the publisher should bear in mind just what the retail price of the book should, ideally be. This is determined on the basis of probable costs of manufacture as well as the prices of similar books meant for the same market. For example, if the length of the book and the material to be included in it are such that it would have to bear a retail price of twenty dollars, the publisher, before agreeing to publish the book, must be certain that there actually is a market for such a book at so high a price.

These conclusions are relatively easy to reach. Probable cost can be roughly estimated by past experience

May we please have a rough estimate for TRUDY'S STRAW HAT. Tentative
specs are as follows:

32 pages

9 3/4 x 9 trim size

Three color pre-separated artwork throughout (brown line, brown, yellow,
and blue halftones). The jacket will be the same with art on the front
and on the back.

Paper — 80 lb. Paloma Matte

Ends — Multicolored textured

Cloth — GSB

Stamping — Ink (the artist will prepare a die for the front cover)

Library Binding

Composition costs will be approximately $500

Quantity — 7,500 copies

Retail Price — $5.95–$6.95

Information furnished by editor (above) for preparation of rough estimate (at right); costs represented on per copy basis include only expenses for production and royalty and do not allow for general overhead

PLANT COST

COMP	AA's	
	Text *Comp + Stats*	$500
	Capts.	
	Index, rh, heads, misc.	
	Repros	
	Jkt. fronts & flaps	
ART	Text design	100.00
	Text mech. *paste type on mech*	32.00
	Jackets *die mech*	40.00
PREP	Camera & Plates	1350.00
	Strip illus. *Semi press proofing*	400.00
	Make Ready	
	Shoot line & h.t.	
	Jkt. prep, proof	210.00
	~~Jkt. final pl. & blue~~ *Proof paper see back*	80.00
	Cov. final pl. & blue	
	Color seps. & pfs.	
	Insert strip & pl.	
	Stats & blues	
MISC	Dies	
	Slipcase/Box/Mech. Bds.	
	Other	$2712
	TOTAL PLANT	

SHEET COST	Text paper *Gould 1513*	
	Text pw & slit *United $370*	
	Insert paper	
	Insert pw	
	End pw & stock	
	Jkt. pw & stock *prints 2up with text.*	
	Cov. pw & stock	
	Lam. film/liq.	
	Sheet freight *$150*	
	Bind—FOB Avenel	
	TOTAL MFG. COST	
	Storage	
	ROYALTY RATE *10%*	
	TOTAL COST *per copy*	

OK _____ From _____

Title TRUDY'S STRAW HAT

ISBN #: Cloth _____ Paper _____

Price: $5.95/$6.95 Cloth _____ Paper _____

Trim 9 3/4 x 9 Text Pages 32 Forms 2/sw

Illustration Pages _____ 2 Jackets Forms

Halftones 3 DROPOUTS, 1 Line shot per page.

Text # Colors 3 COLORS Imposition _____

Paper 42 x 58 ; 80 # 410/M _____ 1"

Paloma Matte.

7.5 M 9000 Sheets 3690 # @ .4100

_____ M _____ Sheets _____ @ _____

_____ M _____ Sheets _____ @ _____

Binding Specs _____ Bindery (Keenan)

Sewing Side Lining _____

Text # Page/Sig 2/16's Back Flat

Boards .088 Binders Ends Multicolor/colored

Stamp Ink R Bands _____

Cloth GSB

~~Illustrations~~ Bind As 11 x 18 Poster space available

QUANTITY	QUANTITY	QUANTITY
7500	7500	
$5.95 retail	$6.95 retail	
.3616		
.2018		
.1827		
.0200		
.6000		
1.3660	1.3660	
.0300	.0300	
.5950	.6950	
1.9911	$2.0910	

with books of similar length and types of material to be included, such as illustrations. Prices of similar books on the market can be easily determined through a survey made by the sales department—or, for that matter, by anyone who carefully browses through a bookstore. There are some things that a publisher knows from experience: a medium-length novel cannot be sold for more than a given price; an illustrated biography or work of history can be sold for a higher price than the novel could; a highly specialized work meant for a limited market (which will, out of necessity, buy the book at almost any price) is able to carry a high retail price. The publisher knows, too, that a high retail price can even be advantageous in the case of what is essentially a gift book, a book that is often called a "coffee table" book since it is frequently shown off—on a coffee table—rather than read.

Retail price will depend, too, on the number of copies to be printed, a projection that can be made by the sales and editorial departments. While it is true that the more copies printed the less each single copy of a book will cost, it would be foolish to print a large number of copies of a title merely to bring the retail price down when it is clear that that number of copies cannot be sold. It makes no sense to produce ten thousand copies of a book in order to obtain a low cost, when only five thousand can reasonably be expected to sell. In addition, because of increasing inventory costs—the costs of holding unsold books in the warehouse—publishers must determine how many copies can be sold over a given period of time. A first printing should be based on projected sales over a twelve month (or, at most, eighteen month) period to be economically sound.

This decision is an extremely important one and whenever possible should be determined in advance. It is here that the greatest risks in publishing a book occur and at this point that a publisher's knowledge of his market is of greatest importance. No publisher is always right, no matter how good his instincts or advice, but as good a guess as possible must be made—on the basis of previous experience with similar books, or books by the same author, as well as on a publishing house's judgment of a book's commercial appeal. It is a tricky decision, and it might well be revised before a book is actually published. Today the public may be interested in astrology, but by the time the book on astrology is published the public's interest could have waned, or else there might already be too many competing books on the same subject. Readers' interests change, and most publishers are eager to follow trends. All too often, a publisher will commission or sign up a book on a subject that seems appealing—only to find, several months later when the book is ready to be sold, that several other volumes on the same subject have already appeared or are about to appear. No publisher, no sales or editorial department can be sure that a given number of copies of any title should be printed. Determination of the size of the printing is a guess based on experience and intuition of the needs of the reader; the commercial success or failure of any book depends greatly on the accuracy of that guess.

Other basic decisions can, at least tentatively, be made before a publisher finally commits himself to the publication of a book, and these decisions will concern the manner in which the book will be physically presented—thus affecting cost and retail price. The trim size—the size of the pages of the book after they have been cut open—can be determined through the nature of the material. Costs as well as aesthetics must be constantly kept in mind while making this decision, which has been made easier in modern times with the increasing degree of standardization of book sizes. An average novel or small work of nonfiction will usually have a trim size of 5⅜ by 8¼ inches; a larger novel or a large work of nonfiction will be somewhat bigger—5½ by 8¼; and a major work of nonfiction or a book that is to be heavily illustrated may be 6⅛ by 9¼. These are more or less standard sizes that will apply to most books, but there are also very many exceptions to these rules, above all for children's books, art books, and those coffee table books whose appeal might be enhanced by an unusual size.

A book can be any size that the publisher wants it to be, and a special or unusual format could be an attractive selling point—but all concerned must realize that an unusual format will raise the price of a book. It is clearly advisable to determine well in advance whether or not this novel presentation of a volume will be feasible or advisable.

Another factor that could weigh heavily on a publishing house's decision—both on whether to accept the book and on the eventual contract terms if that book is accepted—is the need for illustrations and the nature of the illustrations. Illustrations are expensive, whether they be original artwork or photographs. Once the original cost of their procurement has been paid, they are expensive to reproduce. This is especially true in the case of color illustrations. The use of color rather than black and white can drastically alter the cost of a book and thus its retail price. Because of this, a publisher must take great care in deciding just how many illustrations—color, and black and white—are necessary for any given book, and how many can be allowed. If a book absolutely needs a certain number of illustrations, and the costs involved in reproducing and printing these illustrations are excessive, the publisher will either have to reject the book or adjust the terms of the contract.

By the same token, a publisher must take into consideration costs of translation for a work not originally written in the English language. These costs are high—justifiably so, since translation is a difficult and time-consuming job—but because of them a publisher could either be forced to reject a book or offer the author a lower royalty scale in his contract.

Obviously, many factors are involved in deciding

Der Hochleistungssport unserer Zeit scheint dem echten Außenseiter kaum noch eine Chance zu lassen. So groß meist die Startfelder in den einzelnen Wettbewerben gerade bei Olympischen Spielen sind, die Sieger kommen fast ausnahmslos aus einem kleinen Favoritenkreis. Sapporo hat jedoch wieder einmal gezeigt, daß Überraschungen auch heute noch möglich sind. Gerade sie geben dem Sport immer wieder Spannung und neue Würze.

Besonders zwei Außenseitersiege machten das deutlich. Ein bis dahin kaum hervorgetretener Pole, der nur als Ersatzmann den Flug nach Japan angetreten hatte, gewann den Sprunglauf von der Großschanze. Wojciech Fortuna machte seinem Namen alle Ehre. Ihm lachte das olympische Glück und trug ihn auf goldene Weiten.

Als nicht weniger sensationell kann der Erfolg des spanischen Slalom-Wunders Ochoa gewertet werden. Der Hotelierssohn aus der Sierra Nevada oberhalb Granadas gab der gesamten Weltelite das Nachsehen. Spanien hatte seinen ersten Sieger bei Olympischen Winterspielen. Neben diesen großen Sensationen gab es noch mehr triumphierende Außenseiter. So etwa die deutsche Eisschnelläuferin Monika Pflug.

Nicht immer muß es gleich Gold sein, um von einem Erfolg eines Außen-

From a book submitted to an American publisher by a German publisher

whether or not a manuscript should be accepted for publication, just as special factors must be taken into consideration when offering terms for a contract. Fortunately, for the author, each publisher can reach different conclusions, so that a manuscript may be rejected by several houses and still taken on by another.

Once the publisher has decided to take on a work, he offers the author or the author's agent—or sometimes a qualified lawyer—a contract. This rather complicated agreement binds the author to the publisher, setting the rules that will be followed by both parties as long as the book is in print.

A contract to publish a book is a long document, far too involved according to some authors, yet it is undoubtedly better to have more, rather than fewer, rules carefully defined. In this way, misunderstandings are more easily avoided in the future, and each partner to the agreement is more certain of his rights.

Briefly, a contract defines the commitments to be taken by both the author and the publisher, and it establishes the financial terms therein.

Under the terms of the agreement, the author grants to the publisher the exclusive right to publish his work over a set period of time within a given territory. In return for this right, the publisher in almost all cases pays the author an advance—a guarantee—against a royalty. A royalty is a percentage of the retail price of the book. In other words, the publisher might pay an author an advance of two thousand dollars against a royalty of 10 percent for a certain number of copies sold, 12½ percent for a fixed number of additional copies sold, and 15 percent for any copies sold above that number. The advance is "against" royalty: for example, if the publisher has paid an advance of two thousand dollars, the author receives no further payment until he has earned that amount from his royalties. If the book sells for ten dollars, he would receive one dollar for each book sold, so that no more money would be due to him until the book had sold two thousand copies. After that, he receives one dollar for each copy sold, until he reaches a sale of, say, five thousand copies. At that point, his royalty—or percentage—increases to 12½ percent, and he will begin earning one dollar and twenty-five cents

Contract

AGREEMENT made the nineteenth **day of** March , 19 73 ,

between Tamara Hovey , whose

address is 10 Avenue de l'Observatoire, Paris 14, France hereinafter

referred to as the "Author," and Crown Publishers, Incorporated

of 419 Park Avenue South, New York, New York, hereinafter referred to as the "Publisher," with respect to the work tentatively entitled JOHN REED: A BIOGRAPHY

hereinafter referred to as the "Work."

1. The Author hereby grants to the Publisher, its successors and assigns, during the term of the copyrights in the Work and all renewals and extensions thereof as presently in force or as hereafter amended by law:

(a) The exclusive right to print, publish and sell the Work and to cause the Work to be printed, published and sold in book form in the English language in the United States of America, its present territories and possessions, the Republic of the Philippines, and Canada, and the non-exclusive similar right to sell the same in all countries throughout the world except the (British) Commonwealth of Nations (exclusive of Canada) as presently constituted;

(b) The exclusive right to publish or license the work for publication in the English language in the (British) Commonwealth of Nations (exclusive of Canada); but if the Work has not been so published or licensed for publication or is not under option for such publication within eighteen (18) months after first publication of the Work in the United States, then the Author may rescind the right granted in this subdivision (b), by written notice delivered to the Publisher;

(c) The exclusive right to license the Work for publication in any other language throughout the world, but as to each country and language in which the Work has not been so licensed for publication, or is not under option for such publication within three (3) years after first publication of the Work in the United States, the Author may rescind by written notice to the Publisher the right granted as to such country and language included in this subdivision (c).

2. The Author warrants that the Work is not in the public domain, that he is the sole author of the Work, and the owner of all the rights in this agreement granted to the Publisher or in which the Publisher has an interest hereunder and has full power and authority to enter into this agreement; that the Work is original with the Author in every respect; that neither the Work nor any part thereof has heretofore been published except as follows (here include permissions acquired by the Author for the Work, if any):

that the Author has not heretofore granted any rights in the Work except as hereinabove set forth and as follows:

The Author agrees that he will notify the Publisher promptly in writing of any arrangement that he may make in connection with the Work prior to the first publication of the Work hereunder, and secure copyright protection therefor in the United States, Canada, and such other countries in which the Work may be published, and will also notify the Publisher of all copyrights in the Work or any part thereof that may hereafter be secured and will deliver to the Publisher timely, recordable assignments to the Publisher of all such United States copyrights. Prior publication of the Work in any form shall be licensed by the Author only with the written consent of the Publisher, and such prior publication shall not exceed 50% of the Work.

3. The Author warrants that the Work does not infringe any copyright or violate any other right of any person or party whatsoever and does not contain any defamatory, libelous or unlawful matter. The Author agrees to hold the Publisher harmless against any loss, damage, expense (including legal fees), judgments and decrees which the Publisher may suffer or incur as the result of the assertion of any claim or the commencement of any action or proceeding against the Publisher upon the ground that the Work contains any defamatory, libelous or other unlawful matter or infringes upon any copyright or violates any other right of any person or party whatsoever, or as a result of undertaking the defense of any such claim, action or proceeding against any of the Publisher's licensees or purchasers of the Work, and the payment of any judgment rendered therein, or any settlement therefore, if any. In the event that any such claim, action or proceeding is instituted, the Publisher shall promptly notify the Author and may withhold payments due him under this or any other agreement with the Publisher until any payment of a claim or settlement is made.

4. The author shall deliver to the Publisher not later than January 1, 1974, ~~months after the date of this agreement~~ a legible typewritten or printed copy of the Work, in form and substance satisfactory and acceptable to the Publisher, complete and ready for the printer, together with material from which such illustrations, ~~maps and diagrams~~ as the parties may jointly deem necessary ~~and be reproduced without redrawing for use in the volume herein contemplated~~ collectively hereinafter referred to as the "Manuscript." If the Author shall fail to deliver such Manuscript to the Publisher by the said date of delivery, upon notice to

First page of a publisher's negotiated contract

for each copy sold. When he reaches a sale of, say, ten thousand copies, that percentage might go up to 15 percent of the retail price—or one dollar and a half for each copy sold.

It is important that an author understand that the financial division between author and publisher is not out of proportion as it might seem. The publisher spends a great deal of money editing, manufacturing, promoting, and selling a book; in addition, each book is sold to stores at a discount—the store too must make a profit—and this discount averages approximately 43 percent of the retail price.

In addition to the royalty paid to the author on the number of books sold, the publisher agrees to pay the author a certain percentage of other rights—called subsidiary rights. However, if the author is agented, the agent will keep some of these rights. Subsidiary rights include sales to paperback houses for inexpensive reprint, rights to excerpt in textbooks and anthologies, book club rights, movie rights, translations into foreign languages, serialization in newspapers and magazines, and many more.

Most important, of course, the publisher through this contract agrees to print and publish the work in the best possible way, while the author guarantees that the work is his own and agrees to furnish all materials necessary to the completion of the book—a bibliography, an index, a glossary, and so on, if any of these is required.

This is the beginning of a partnership between author

and publisher. They will be working together, and it is in the interest of both parties that the book is published well and successfully—that the author's aims in writing the book are faithfully carried out in its manufacture and presentation, and that the largest possible number of copies are sold. As with any business partnership, however, these complicated and detailed rules must be established at the beginning, and the responsibilities of each partner defined as clearly as possible before the actual partnership becomes effective.

The Editor

When an author's manuscript is accepted for publication, it is assigned to an editor—almost always the man or woman who acquired the manuscript for the publishing house. At that point, it is the editor's function to work with that manuscript and the author. The editor becomes the author's intermediary between the work he has done by himself and the public that he hopes to reach.

Nonetheless, an editor's job involves far more than editing. Above all, he must be in close touch with what is being written—not only in the United States but throughout the world. He must read newspapers and magazines, getting from them ideas for books. He must keep his eyes open for new talent, reading short stories wherever they appear as a possible lead to a new and promising author. A good short story published in a magazine by a previously unknown writer will almost always bring a letter from a book editor, asking to see more of the author's work, in the hopes that a book could develop. The editor discovers talent and encourages it wherever he finds it.

Part of the editor's job is to keep in contact with literary agents, obtaining from them the works of their most promising authors. The editor solicits manuscripts and reads and evaluates *all* those that come to his attention, unsolicited as well as solicited. The editor's job does not end when he leaves his office; he is constantly on the lookout for new books and new ideas, and, in the case of an idea that seems suitable for a book, he must be able to find the proper author to write that book. Commissioned books, which develop from an idea which is born in a publishing house, often make up a substantial part of a publisher's list, and it is largely the task of an editor to come up with such ideas.

All of this is important, yet the editor's main job is to edit, and the relationship between editor and author, at least in the several months preceding publication of the book, is a very special and close one. The author has been alone with his manuscript for months or even years. It might have been shown to a wife or husband or friend, but it is most likely that no one has read it as critically, as closely, or as objectively as the editor will. Indeed, if the editor does his job well, he must absorb every part of that manuscript and give it his most careful and sympathetic attention.

Obviously, the role of the editor is an extremely important one in the making of a book, and it must not be underestimated. Nor, on the other hand, should it be overestimated. It is romantic to read of an editor acting as a constant companion, a kind of psychoanalyst to an author, but this rarely happens. The editor is a professional aid, but not more than that. There have been relationships between editors and authors that have become legends. Such and such author, we hear, could never have written as well as he did had it not been for his sensitive editor who held his hand during nights of insomnia or rescued him from lengthy drinking bouts, and so on. Undoubtedly, some editors have established unusually close and personal relationships with some authors, but an editor cannot "make" an author a success, just as he happily lacks the power to make him a failure.

The editor's main responsibility is to work on manuscripts; his importance to any given author is not that of a close friend or psychiatrist, but as a constructive critic. His role is to see if there might be any way in which a manuscript could be improved and to recognize its defects as well as its value. He will suggest improvements to the author but will not make them himself—he is not the writer. In the end, an intelligent editor knows he must respect the author's wishes, for the book will, after all, be published under the name of the author, who is the one to assume final responsibility.

Each editor works in his own way, but most probably

Thank you very much for sending along SCARY SARY AND THE SNUFFBOX.
We think it is an entertaining story that would appeal to children
in the middle elementary grades, both in terms of the excitement
generated by the plot and the problem of fear that it involves.
The story isn't filled out enough, however, especially in terms
of its main character, Sara. In addition, the reader is too convinced
of the ultimate success that Sara will have for the suspense to be
truly engrossing. We're hoping that you will want to revise along
those lines.

I'd like to make some general remarks about what seems to be lacking
in your treatment of Sara. She has the makings of a very believable
and individual character, but at this point she is still too much
in your hands. The reader's relationship to her is almost cinematic--
at just those places where we want to be inside of her, to know
explicitly what she is feeling and thinking, how her mind is racing
when she's trying to save the bread and snuffbox, we have a long
range, distant view of what she is doing. We see her, but we are
not with her. This results in the simplification of Sara's fear--
we know she's afraid, but we really don't know the inside, the
specifics of that fear. Is she afraid of being weak? of being over-
powered? of giving in instead of fighting? Is she afraid of the
feeling of fear? Does she just lack confidence? Is she ashamed of
feeling afraid? None of this needs to be spelled out, but her
psychology must be firmly felt by you, so that her responses and
the various scenes in your story become more individuated. What is
that part of Sara like that comes forward to show her that she
can do what she doesn't believe she can do? Does she talk to
herself, urge herself on? Does she take her brother Ezra or her
father, or even her grandfather as a model? Has she perhaps in fact
been brave at other times in her life, but doesn't really believe
in them?

We are not continuously enough in touch with Sara's sense impressions,
and because this whole journey is entirely new to her, it seems natural
that her observations and feelings would be full and keen, and fun
for her despite her fear.

--continued--

First page of an editor's letter to a prospective author

he will read the manuscript as a whole to get an overall picture of the work. At this point, he will be watching for general organization, for improvements that might be achieved by reorganization of the manuscript. This could mean a rearrangement of chapters, or the lengthening or tightening of certain sections. In a novel, this could mean the further development of certain characters or even the elimination of some others; it might mean clarifying the motivations that lead to certain acts. In a biography, the editor could suggest additional material about a certain phase of the subject's life or a certain period in it. All of these imply relatively major changes, and, as a result, serious discussions and exchanges of ideas with the author. A good editor never tries to dictate; he suggests, as persuasively but as tactfully as possible, for authors are, with good reason, sensitive about their work.

Once these major changes have been discussed, the editor should read the manuscript a second time, after which he will be far more specific. He looks for factual errors, for unclear sentences, phrases that seem to him trite or overused. He makes certain that the author has really said what he has wanted to, and he catches inconsistency in logic or characterization. If the editor does not overextend his role, and respects the individuality of the author, the latter will be more than grateful for any corrections or suggestions. Even the most careful author might say on one page that a character has blue eyes and on a later page that he has brown eyes; he

Ellen dreaded that trip to the pump ~~so much she could~~ ~~hardly make herself get ready to start~~. It would be good to stay in the safe warm kitchen and never go out.

~~There was now~~ a crackling fire on the hearth ~~which~~ made bright lights on the copper pans and on the blue china plates in the cupboard. It made the quilt ~~coverlet~~ on the big bed look like a field of bluebells, and shone on ~~It picked out of the shadows overhead~~ the bunches of dried herbs that hung from the rafters shadowy overhead.

Ellen looked around. "This kitchen makes me feel happy," she said.

"It makes me happy, too," Mother said wistfully.

"I used to sew and knit with my mother here by the fire. ~~And~~ she taught me my lessons here at this ~~same~~ big table by this very window."

An edited manuscript page

might describe a sofa as green on one page and as red on another. He might well believe, too, that he has made his point only to find that by following an editor's suggestion he will make it even more clearly.

Depending on the specific nature of the book, the editor has further responsibilities. If there are to be photographs, he must see to it that they are placed properly in the text and that precise and accurate captions have been provided for them. If the book is a picture book for children, the editor will devote a great deal of time to the illustrator, making sure that the illustrations complement and extend the story.

An editor's job can be an immensely satisfying one, to which he brings a broad cultural background, a knowledge of literature, and, above all, a love of books. By the

Captions keyed to photographs

```
                frontispiece (no caption)

photo #1:   F. Scott Fitzgerald

photo #1a:    "    "        "

photo #2:   Fitzgerald's mother, Mary McQuillan Fitzgerald

photo #3:   The house in St. Paul, Minnesota as it appeared in 1916,
            when Fitzgerald lived there

photo #4:   Fitzgerald at age three, with his father, Edward Fitzgerald
            Christmas 1899

photo #5:   Fitzgerald at sixteen

photo #6:   Ariel view of Princeton University

photo #7:   John Peale Bishop as a Princeton undergraduate

photo #8:   The cover of the musical score, Fie! Fie! Fi-Fi. Fitzgerald
            wrote the lyrics as well as the book for the Triangle Club's
            production
```

time the editor and author (and illustrator, in some cases) have finished working together, most editorial problems should have been solved.

There does, however, remain one job: the preparation of the front and back matter—that is, the pages that come before the actual beginning of the text and after the end of that text.

These pages serve to give us more information about the book. The very first page will usually carry the name of the book, and it is called the half title, or the bastard. The next page might be blank or it might have a map or illustration. The third page contains the title of the book as well as the name of the author, that of the publisher, and sometimes the date and place of publication. The fourth page is the copyright page, the page on which a copyright notice (the legal claim that the author or publisher, usually the former, makes to the work) is placed, as well as the Library of Congress Cataloging in Publication Data and, often, printing information. The following page has the dedication, if the volume is dedicated to someone, and this is followed by a table of contents. If there are illustrations in the book, a list of illustrations will follow. After that will come a foreword, preface, acknowledgments, and an introduction, if any or all of these are to be included in the book. After these introductory pages, another half title is placed (this will be a part title if the book is divided into parts). That will be on a right-hand page; the reverse side is almost always blank and is generally followed by

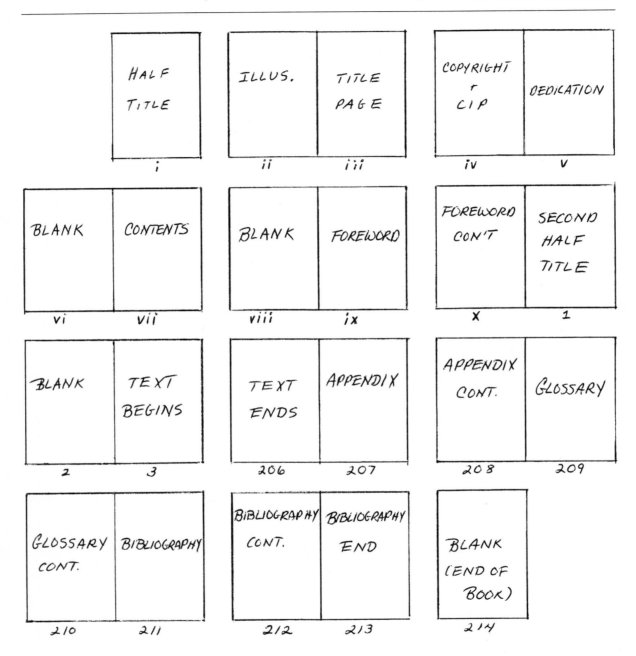

HALF TITLE	
i	

ILLUS.	TITLE PAGE
ii	iii

COPYRIGHT r CIP	DEDICATION
iv	v

BLANK	CONTENTS
vi	vii

BLANK	FOREWORD
viii	ix

FOREWORD CON'T	SECOND HALF TITLE
x	1

BLANK	TEXT BEGINS
2	3

TEXT ENDS	APPENDIX
206	207

APPENDIX CONT.	GLOSSARY
208	209

GLOSSARY CONT.	BIBLIOGRAPHY
210	211

BIBLIOGRAPHY CONT.	BIBLIOGRAPHY END
212	213

BLANK (END OF BOOK)
214

Sample plan for flow of front and back matter for a 224 page book the beginning of the text itself. If all of these introductory pages are not ready by the time the manuscript leaves the editorial department—and this often happens—the fact that they are to come must be noted as an aid to the designer.

The same is true for the back matter, which follows the text. This will include appendices and notes, supplementary material that will aid in understanding the text itself; a glossary—a definition of various terms used in the book; a bibliography—a list of books or articles used in researching the book, as well as of books that will be useful for further reading on the subject; and an index. The latter, of course, cannot be compiled until the book has actually been divided into pages.

The editor's major jobs, then, are finished, and the manuscript should be almost ready to be turned into a book. But before its initial stages of production and design, this manuscript must be carefully worked on by another kind of editor—this one is called the copy editor.

There is one notable exception to this rule, and that is the picture book for very young children in which the role of the illustrator is equal in importance to that of the author of the text, but the role of the illustrator will be fully discussed in the following chapter.

Before the manuscript is turned over to the copy editor, a manuscript transmittal form is prepared by the editor, and a copy of this all-important form is sent not only to the copy editor but to the designer and to the

MANUSCRIPT TRANSMITTAL FORM

Title __The Good Old Summertime__
Author __Floyd and Marion Rinhart__
Editor __JP/JW__
# of pages wanted __320__
Quantity __7,500__
Imprint __Clarkson N. Potter, Inc.__
Trim size __8½ x 11__

Date __June 29, 1976__
Tent. price __$14.95 firm__
Bound books wanted __February 1977__
Pub. date __April 1, 1977__
Designer __SD__
Production Supervisor __MF__
Age group __Adult__

Front Matter: # of pp. (Roman/Arabic)

Half title	__i__
Card page	
Title	__iii__
Copyright	__iv__
Acknowl.	__vii-viii__
Dedication	
Contents	__v-vi__
Perface	
Foreword	
Intro.	__ix-x__
List of Illus.	
Other	

Text:
Ms. pages __210__

Back Matter:

Appendix	__to come__
Glossary	
Biblio	__to come__
Index	__to come__

Sample pp. wanted __yes__

Sample pp OK'd by __JP/JW__

Special Matter:
Illustrations: __393 black and white__
Frontis __yes__ halftones
Endpapers _____
Captions __to come__

Extracts:
Letters _____
Poetry __yes p. 87__
Quotes _____
Others __excerpts: pp. 33-37__
__120-126__
__189-200__

Running Heads:
Left __part title__
Right __chapter title__

Text Heads:
Part titles __A heads__
Chapter titles __B heads__
Chapter Numbers _____
  arabic _____
  roman _____
Main heads __C heads__
Sub-heads __D heads__
Sub-sub heads __E heads__
Other _____

Folios:
With R.H. __yes__
Separate _____

Jacket:

Art __to come__
Blurb __to come__
Back ad _____
Photo _____

Binding Stamp copy:
__to come__

Remarks & Special Treatment:

Proof Requirements:
Galleys:
  edit. __1 master, 2 duplicates__
  other __2 bound galleys__
Pages __1 master, 2 duplicates__

Reading time (approximate):
Galleys __2 weeks__

Pages __1 week__

production department as well. This form is a summary of all the information on hand and will be used as a guide throughout the various stages of the book's production.

Included on the form are the title of the book, the names of the author and the editor, the number of pages wanted, the number of books to be printed, the trim size, and the tentative price. In addition, there is the name of the designer, and of the production supervisor, the date on which finished books are wanted, and the proposed date of publication.

The editor provides, too, every possible detail concerning the manuscript. This includes a list of what makes up the front matter and what makes up the back matter—noting what material is already on hand and what is to come. There is a list of special matter to be included that is not part of the text: illustrations, frontispiece, endpapers, captions, graphs, charts, and so on. A note has to be made of the extent of any special matter in the text, as well as a list of chapter and part titles, main heads, subheads, sub-subheads—and the precise nature and importance of these. Mention must be made of running heads, those single lines on the tops of pages which run throughout the book as an aid to the reader.

Proof requirements, too, are noted on this form—just how many sets of proofs are required, and approximately how long will be needed to read them. Finally, there must be information about the jacket—the artwork as well as the written material—and about exactly what must be printed on the book's cover.

When the editor has summarized all this information, the manuscript is ready to be copy-edited; after that, it will be designed and put into production. A great deal has been done, but the job of making a book is little less than half completed.

To: Ginny   **Date:** November 4, 1974

From: NJS

Re: THEY CAME TO PARIS by Howard Greenfeld

Herewith the above manuscript for copy editing along with the manuscript transmittal forms. The index is missing; otherwise it is complete. I would greatly appreciate it if JC could copy edit this; she knows the period well. Many thanks.

Memo from an editor to the copy editing department

The Illustrator

Just as writers express themselves through words, illustrators express themselves by means of pictures. Until recent times, a large number of books were illustrated, notably novels and short stories. These illustrated books—with the exception of some works done by well-known artists in gift editions—are no longer in fashion, and the illustrator today will be, for the most part, called upon to illustrate books for children.

It is often out of their experience from books seen and read during childhood that many illustrators develop their interest in art. Instinctively, many children find greater pleasure and satisfaction in the pictures that accompany the stories they read than they do from the words that convey those stories. They then find themselves drawing rather than writing in order to express themselves, and it is precisely this interest in pictorial representation that leads many men and women to

choose book illustration as a career.

Unlike the writer, however, in most cases the illustrator needs special training to pursue his or her career. Techniques and craftsmanship must be learned—either through years of full-time study at an art school or at least through a course of part-time studies. The illustrator, of necessity, must have an expert knowledge of drawing and of the various mediums of artistic expression. A knowledge of the history of art and of the various schools of art is also important. Important, too, is a good knowledge of printing so that he or she may best know how to prepare the artwork for the printer. Above all, however, the illustrator is an artist: he or she must have an eye and a vivid imagination.

The problems that an illustrator faces in finding a publisher for his work are somewhat different from those that face the writer. The illustrator must have something to illustrate, and unless he has illustrated a story that he himself has written, which is sometimes the case, it is an editor or art director who will ask him to illustrate a story which has been written by someone else. For this reason, the inexperienced illustrator in search of work would be best advised to prepare a portfolio of drawings he has done; this could include a story that he has illustrated as a sample on his own initiative. Obviously, any previously published work, too, should be included in that portfolio, which will be shown to the right person at the publishing house. Whether the right person to see is the children's book

Illustrations from Diane de Groat's portfolio

editor or the art director depends on the structure of the house, but in most houses the editor will be more useful for the editor is the person who knows first what books will be published that might be best suited to the style of a particular illustrator.

It is from the portfolio that the editor or art director will have a clear idea of the kind of book that an illustrator can best illustrate. If there is nothing on hand that seems suitable for an illustrator who shows talent, the editor or art director will keep his or her name on file, making a note of that illustrator's special style and skills. Coincidence and luck, thus, play a part: it is entirely possible, for example, that an artist with a particular style (and if the artist can work in several different styles, he or she should have samples of each in the

Illustrations from John Wallner's portfolio

portfolio) might walk into an editor's office on the very day that the editor has decided to publish a manuscript suited to his or her talents.

This might happen, just as it might not. For an experienced editor or art director working with illustrated books, each manuscript will generate a certain feeling that will lead that editor or art director to visualize to some extent the kind of art that will be required. It might be funny or serious, modern or traditional; it might call for bright colors, or it might call for soft colors. On the basis of the story, the editor or art director can begin to see the whole book. Thus, the editor or art director will have a basic idea of the kind of art the story demands before he or she looks for an illustrator. The choice is large, since, unlike writers, illustrators sometimes work for several houses. Too, some artists work quickly and can do two books a year, while others work more slowly. (No publisher can guarantee that he will publish enough books suited to one illustrator's style over a given period of time.)

For this reason, editors and art directors must not only look for new talent, but must also be aware of the work of illustrators who have already been published and be able to recognize that one illustrator's style would fit a given story. They will know an artist's overall style, sense of characterization, and his or her use of color and detail.

The editor or art director will then submit the story to the chosen, potential illustrator. If that illustrator does not like the story or have a feeling for it, he or she should turn it down. If, however, the illustrator likes the story and wants to illustrate it, preliminary discussions with the editor will follow the reading. After these, if the artist has been published before, it is time to draw up a contract; if, on the other hand, the artist is unknown, he or she will most likely be asked to prepare a sample illustration before going ahead with the contract. In fairness to the artist, no editor or art director should ever ask more than one illustrator to sample the same story at the same time.

If the sample is acceptable, the contract can then be drawn up; if it is nearly acceptable, more discussion and revision are called for. If, however, the sample seems hopeless, the editor or art director is forced to reject it

/Artist 4. The/author shall deliver to the Publisher not later than Nov. 1, 1972 months after the date of this agreement a legible typewritten or printed copy of the Work, in form and substance satisfactory and acceptable to the Publisher, complete and ready for the printer, twenty black-
/and-white together with material from which such illustrations, maps and diagrams as the parties may
/which jointly deem necessary can be reproduced without redrawing for use in the volume herein Tales of Mr.
/Pengachoosa contemplated, collectively hereinafter referred to as the "Manuscript." If the/Author shall /Artist
/illustrations fail to deliver such/Manuscript to the Publisher by the said date of delivery, upon notice to
/Artist/Artist the/Author, the/Author shall repay to the Publisher the amount of any advance theretofore
/Artist received by the/Author hereunder. If, in the opinion of the Publisher, the/text is not, because /illustrations
of inaccuracy of grammar, spelling, punctuation, capitalization or the like, ready for the /are not
/Artist printer, the Publisher may request the/Author to make necessary corrections, and if the Au-
/Artist thor within four weeks after such request shall fail to deliver the Manuscript corrected/as /illustrations
aforesaid, then the Publisher may have the necessary corrections made and the cost resulting
/for from a reading thereof and/making the necessary corrections shall be paid by the/Author /Artist
upon rendition of invoice or upon the option of the Publisher be charged against any sums
/Artist accruing to the/Author under the terms of this agreement.

5. The Author agrees to read, revise, correct and promptly return all proof sheets of the Work; and the cost of alterations, in type or in plates, required by the Author other than those due to printer's errors, in excess of 10% of the cost of composition shall be paid by the Author upon rendition of invoice or upon the option of the Publisher be charged against any sums accruing to the Author under the terms of this agreement. If such proof sheets be not promptly returned, the Publisher may publish the Work as printed therein. If an index to the Work shall be required by the Publisher, the same shall be provided by the Author to the Publisher within 7 days of the receipt of page proofs by the Author; otherwise the Publisher may have such index prepared at the Author's expense.

From a publisher's contract with an illustrator

and look for another illustrator. In order to avoid disappointments of this kind, much thought and consideration must be given before an illustrator is asked to prepare a sample.

Once the editor or art director has chosen the illustrator, it is time to draw up the contract, one that will—because of the different factors involved—differ from that offered to the author.

The crucial factor in this agreement is the balance between art and text. If only a few line drawings or illustrations are called for, the artist will be offered a flat fee. No long, formal contract is necessary in these cases; a letter of agreement indicating the precise number and kinds of illustrations required and the fee to be paid will suffice. The artwork is considered an added touch and not an essential part of these books.

However, when the illustrations are essential, it is up to the editor or art director to assess the importance of these illustrations to the book and draw up a contract which will reflect, in percentages, this assessment. The basic 10 percent royalty applies to all books, so that if, for example, the editor feels that the illustrations are half as important as the text, the illustrator will be offered a royalty of $3\frac{1}{3}$ percent while the author will receive twice that amount. For this reason, it is very important that the editor know just what the relationship of text to art will be before offering a contract—not only to the artist but to the author as well. It would obviously be an error to offer an author 10 percent and then realize that the illustrator too should be receiving a percentage—which would result in a royalty higher than the economically feasible 10 percent.

Contracts for picture books, where text and art are of equal importance, are much simpler. Advances, royalties, and all subsequent payments for subsidiary rights are almost always equally divided between the author and the illustrator.

Once the contract has been signed, the actual work can begin. It is the editor, and not the author, with whom the illustrator will work, for it is the editor who will most likely encourage the artist's own creativity. The editor will at this point discuss with the illustrator the trim size of the book and the number of pages wanted, as well as the number of colors that will be used. In addition, they will discuss the pacing of the book and the balance between illustrations and text. Illustrations require movement and vitality in the same way that text does; they must be carefully paced and must reflect the tensions and climaxes of the text itself. Ideally, the illustrations should be able to stand on their own, should be able to tell the story even without the accompanying text.

The illustrator's first job is to prepare rough thumbnail sketches of the characters—sometimes one will be in color. These are brought to the editor and discussed. After these discussions, the artist prepares a rough dummy—generally in black and white. In some cases, he or she takes a copy of the manuscript (because the type is not yet designed or set), cuts it up, and lays it out on the pages. In other cases, the editor or art director will give the artist a blank dummy with a copy of the text broken up and pasted in it. Sketches of the illustrations are then made in relation to the text.

This initial rough dummy is brought to the editor who studies it carefully, often conferring with other members of the department. The artist is then called in, and there is further discussion. If the suggested revisions are minor, he or she will take this black-and-white dummy back and begin to prepare a rough color dummy; if there are to be extensive revisions, a second rough black-and-white dummy will have to be made before work on the color dummy can proceed.

The procedure for the rough color dummy is essentially the same as that for the previous dummy. Preparation on the part of the artist, this time using color, is followed by discussion—this time more detailed—with the editor or art director. Technical aspects, the use of color, and budgetary restrictions are clarified. It must be remembered, parenthetically, that since not all books for children are works of fantasy, a great deal of research may be required by the illustrator who could be called upon to represent pictorially many periods in history and many places. Studies of costumes of various times or countries, of furnishings, and of landscapes could be essential, and the illustrator might have to spend many hours poring through libraries and museums, finding ideas, and learning details essential to the accurate rendering of his work.

Once the rough color dummy has been accepted, the artist prepares the final artwork with the aid of a layout provided by the production department. This layout gives the exact dimensions of the inside of the book and of the jacket. Color work is prepared in one of two ways: it is either camera-separated by the printer, or it is preseparated by the illustrator. In the former case, the artist prepares his illustrations in color as a painter would. He or she could use one of many ways of expression; different illustrators are more comfortable in different media, and some books call for one medium while others would best be executed in other ways. Pen and ink, watercolor, collage, oil, pencil and oil glazes, gouache, and tempera are among the many media used by book illustrators. These illustrations are then turned over to the printer, whose job—including camera separation—will be discussed in a chapter on the color printer.

However, many illustrators are asked to preseparate their art themselves since this method means a large savings in costs, often enabling the publisher to bring out a book he could not afford to do if the art were camera-separated. Preseparation involves a great deal of careful work, requiring precise technical skills from the illustrator, but excellent results can be obtained if the separations have been accurately prepared.

Separating colors means preparing the art with separate black-and-white copy for each color to be used. The

Illustration from artist's rough dummy

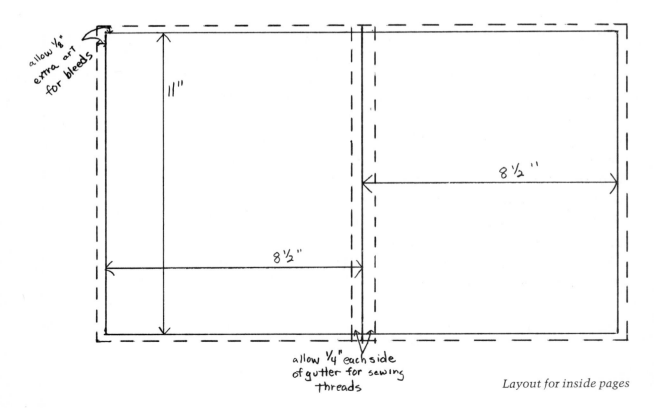

allow ⅛" extra art for bleeds

11"

8 ½ "

8 ½ "

allow ¼" each side of gutter for sewing threads

Layout for inside pages

illustrator, of course, will have been told how many colors can be allowed by the budget and will have to work within those limitations. If four colors are allowed, he can obtain an almost endless number of color tints by combining the four basic colors—black, yellow, blue, and red; if three colors are allowed, there will be fewer, and there will obviously be even fewer possible tints if only two colors can be used.

The illustrator must have a thorough knowledge of color, of what colors result from various mixtures—i.e., blue and yellow produce green, while blue and red produce purple. The artist chooses the colors he will use from among the process colors, particular shades of blue, yellow, red, and black, from which all colors can be obtained. There are several ink companies, each of which publishes a color guide—the most widely used is the Pantone Color Specifier. These color guides show not only the basic shades of the primary colors, but variations of them—some lighter, some darker—that the artist may prefer. The illustrator thus chooses from among these color swatches, or, if he or she finds nothing suitable, he can mix paints as any painter does and produce his own swatches for the printer to match.

Once the colors have been chosen, the illustrator prepares the art for each page of the book. The parts that are to be printed in the most important color—usually black—are placed on a board. This is called the key plate, and it contains the line drawing or outline for the illustration, which gives it definition. The areas for

Preseparated Artwork

Artist's separation for the black plate

Artist's separation for the red plate

Artist's separation for the yellow plate

Artist's separation for the blue plate

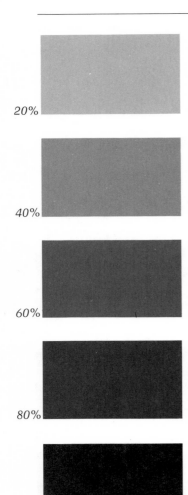

20%

40%

60%

80%

100%

Illustrations above demonstrate gradation of tones from almost white to solid black

other colors are presented on transparent acetate or watercolor-paper overlays that are taped on top of the board. (Watercolor paper is used if a wash effect is wanted.)

The color is indicated on each overlay. For example, the illustrator, after having prepared his black key plate, will mount a piece of acetate with masking tape for his blue plate and proceed to paint (in black) all those areas that should be printed in blue. Once done, he will use the same procedure for the red plate and then for the yellow plate. The overlays for each color plate show only blobs of black—there are no lines—but these blobs show a variation in density. This is because the illustrator has indicated and can obtain light and dark variations of each color he wants, which will determine the density of the color. There are devices by which different screen percentages can be achieved for different parts of the plate and different screen percentages of one color will combine with different screen percentages of another to bring about entirely different results. Tubes of paint which the illustrator may purchase are marked by screen percentages (50% red, 25% yellow, etc.), and the results of the many combinations can be foreseen by the illustrator with the use of color charts.

Another important job for the illustrator in the preparation of the art is to make certain that the register is exact—that is, to see that each overlay is in correct position relative to the key plate and the other overlays. This is achieved by putting register marks on the key plate and on each subsequent overlay and making certain that they align perfectly. Since acetate is transparent, it presents no problem for the illustrator, but when using watercolor paper, the illustrator must mount his overlays over the glass top of a light box, which is illuminated by very strong lights that shine from the bottom.

Before turning in his or her work, the illustrator must carefully check the register as well as the consistency in the density of ink on each page. If, for example, there is a green shirt that recurs throughout the book, it is essential that this green shirt have the same amount of ink on each of the plates showing that shirt.

The illustrator's job is one that obviously calls for technical skills as well as creative ones—most illustrators will even be called upon, and will want, to check their work when the book is on press. Nonetheless, it is a rewarding job: to express through images what a writer has expressed through words, and to see that his or her intentions have been faithfully carried out.

Register marks

The Copy Editor

The reader is never aware of a copy editor's work if the job is well done, but very much aware of it if it has been improperly done. The copy editor is the last person in the editorial department to read a manuscript carefully, and the copy editor's job is a complex and difficult one, requiring intelligence, precision, and care. It is his or her job to check the manuscript for accuracy—in many cases finding errors that the author and editor have overlooked—and to "style" the manuscript. In this case, style does not refer to literary style, but rather spelling, consistency, and usage. The copy editor's most useful tools are a good, comprehensive dictionary and one of several handbooks of style such as *Words into Type* or the University of Chicago Press's *A Manual of Style*, both of them valuable guides to correct usage. In addition, some publishing houses have their own "house" style, a guide to usage preferred by that one house, usu-

COMMA

5.23   The comma indicates the smallest interruption in continuity of thought or sentence structure. There are a few rules governing its use that have become almost obligatory. Aside from these, the use of the comma is mainly a matter of good judgment, with ease of reading as the end in view.

COMPOUND SENTENCES

5.24   When the clauses of a compound sentence are joined by a conjunction, a comma should be placed before the conjunction unless the clauses are short and closely related:

> The two men quickly bolted the door, but the intruder had already entered through the window.
>
> Everyone present was startled by the news, and several senators who had been standing in the hall rushed into the room to hear the end of the announcement.
>
> Are we really interested in preserving law and order, or are we only interested in preserving our own privileges?
>
> Charles played the guitar and Betty sang.

5.25   In a compound sentence composed of a series of short, independent clauses the last two of which are joined by a conjunction, commas should be placed between the clauses and before the conjunction (see also pars. 5.46, 5.64):

> Harris presented the proposal to the governor, the governor dis-

From A Manual of Style

ally issued in mimeographed form to the copy editors and sometimes to authors who are writing for that house.

The problems that a copy editor encounters are innumerable and often unexpected, for each manuscript is different. Consistency is of fundamental importance, and this entails a great deal of checking back and forth in the manuscript. A few examples of this will best illustrate the scope of the copy editor's job.

Consistent spelling is one example; many words can be spelled more than one way—neither being necessarily right or wrong—and the spelling of each word should be the same throughout the book. Should it be wristwatch or wrist watch, postoperative or post-operative? Capitalization too should be consistent, and with the

```
          The copy editor should weigh heads--A, B, C, and so on
     to the necessary number--for the designer, and xerox those
     pages (for sample page copy) on which typical examples appear.
          Because at the time of copy editing it is not known what
     style the designer will choose for heads, the copy editor
     should always indicate what words are to be capitalized in
     any material that is typed in solid caps or in initial cap
     and lowercase (This is initial cap and lowercase.  This Is
     Caps and Lowercase.).  (Do not bother to mark for capital
     a letter that is typed capital.)
          Either use fliers pasted to manuscript pages for queries
     or separately list pages on which queries appear.
          All cross-references within the text, whether to chapters,
     sections, other footnotes, tables, and so on, should be care-
     fully checked.  Be sure to check all illustration references
```

*Portion of publisher's
notes on "house" style*

aid of a dictionary and stylebook, the copy editor must decide when to use Prime Minister and when to use prime minister, Eighteenth Century or eighteenth century, the General or the general. Dates must be written the same way throughout–November 18, 1975, or 18 November 1975–and a decision must be made whether to represent numbers by figures–32–or by words– thirty-two. The copy editor must make certain that the titles of books will be set in italics–*The Great Gatsby*, for example–and that titles of short stories–"The Rich Boy"–will be set in roman type within quotation marks.

The above are merely a few examples of consistency that a copy editor must watch for. He is also responsible for verifying names, dates, and places–any facts–that might have escaped the attention of the author and editor. In some cases, obviously, an author's expertise has to be taken for granted, and this kind of fact-checking will be unnecessary. In others, and the editor of the book should indicate this to the copy editor, it is wise for the latter to double-check.

In addition to making sure that the style is consistent throughout the manuscript and to the checking of facts, the copy editor's job is that of preparing the manuscript for the designer and compositor. For the latter, the copy editor prepares the manuscript in such a way that all is legible—and correct—so the manuscript can be set. For the designer, the copy editor should indicate all matter that is not straight text, that will have to be designed differently. It may be the copy editor's job to point out such matter as chapter headings and subchapter headings by means of symbols such as A and B, to make special markings that will call the designer's attention to poetry or extracts from other works that should be typeset in a manner different from that of the main body of the text. Footnotes must be checked to see that they are properly placed, and the chapter titles in the table of contents should, of course, correspond to the order and exact name in which they are found in the text. Though this might seem obvious, all too often mistakes are made in this seemingly simple step in the making of a book. It is better to check each detail too carefully than not carefully enough, for corrections that have to be made in proofs are costly.

Copy 6-1

The woven basket, made of bread and used to serve it, has a delightful double meaning. It is probably the object that most people associate with bread-dough art, for craftsmen have been displaying them in quality shops for the past few years.

Bread baskets are made from flat rolled dough, cut into strips for weaving, then shaped either over or within a form (see page 00 for both methods). Forms must be ovenproof bowls or baking pans thoroughly greased with vegetable oil so the dough can be easily removed; they should not have under-cuts or rims that will bake within the dough and prevent sep-arating. It is impractical to line a form with aluminum foil to facilitate separating as the foil wrinkles and leaves the wrinkly impressions in the strips.

An average size basket made over an 8-inch diameter bowl requires about two-thirds of a recipe. Dough should be stiff so the strips do not stretch and tear as they are woven.

When a basket is made over the bottom of an inverted bowl placed on a cookie sheet, the rim is made first and the strips attached to it. The rim that lies flat on the pan is always flat. After baking, it can be decorated by gluing on seeds or objects. It can also be embellished by baking on additional

A copy edited manuscript page

The manuscript is now ready to leave the editorial department. Before it is designed and actually set into type, one precaution might be called for: when there is any possible question of libel, it is best to have the manuscript read by a lawyer.

The Designer

Before a manuscript can be turned into a book, it must be designed. By this we mean that specifications must be given as to how the book should look physically. The alternatives are many, for books differ widely not only in editorial content but in appearance.

Basically, the book designer's job is to carry out visually what the author has done with his words. In order to conceive these visual aspects, the designer must call upon a wide variety of skills. His or her background usually includes study in an art school. The designer must have a sense of color, form, space, and texture; he or she must also have a thorough knowledge of printing and book production, so as to know what is and what is not possible. Since with modern technology almost anything is possible, the designer must be very much aware of the economic consequences of any decision taken—whether or not that decision is within the limits of the budget set for a given book. Above all, perhaps, a designer must realize the function and limits of good book design. If the design is obtrusive, if it calls too much attention to itself as design, then it has not been successfully designed.

Before beginning work, a designer must understand thoroughly the nature of the manuscript to be designed. At the time that he or she is given a job, there will most likely be a preliminary discussion with the editor. Then the manuscript, together with the transmittal form which provides the needed factual information, is turned over to the designer.

A careful reading of the manuscript follows. The designer becomes familiar with its style, the feeling it generates, and the market for which it is being published. During this reading, ideas for design and for possible typefaces will be noted as will any special problems that may be involved. These latter will concern chapter headings, subheads, and notes—and where it would be best to place those notes (at the bottom of the page as footnotes, at the end of each chapter, or at the very end of the entire text).

While interpreting the manuscript accurately, the designer must also keep in mind that the finished book must be attractive and one that can be read as comfortably as possible. When he or she has finished the reading, there is sometimes another discussion with the editor; after this, the designer should have a full understanding of the problems and challenges to be met.

Untitled novel - contemporary fiction
ages 8-10

Trim - 5½ × 8¼"   *144 or 176 pages*

10 chapters - will need display type for chapter
titles and numbers. Running heads are
optional. No subheads.

EXTRACT: diary entries - editor suggests italic
2 poems within text

Illustrations: 10 pen and ink line drawings
and frontispiece

Designer's notes

---

t

t   t   t

t   t

t

Lowercase t's from several
different typefaces

Roman

Italic

The designer's first important decision concerns the selection of a typeface from those available at the compositor who will be setting the book. To most readers, it might seem that all the letters which make up the words of all books are the same: a "t" is always a "t." In a sense, this is correct since almost all words are printed in what we call roman letters or italic letters, the latter being slanted to show emphasis or designate special categories such as book titles. However, upon close examination of several books, it will become clear that there are many different styles of type within the overall classification of roman and italic. Type design is a complicated and painstaking art that involves not only considerations of aesthetic beauty, but also a careful study of the combination and compatibility of an alphabet of letters as well as of numbers and punctuation marks. Many typefaces, such as Caslon and Baskerville, are named after their creators.

The differences among the many kinds of typefaces can be noted by examining carefully each letter; what may seem to be the same is often not. A letter is made up of various parts. Some have an upper stroke, called the ascender (as in "d"), and some have a downward stroke, called the descender (as in "y"); there is sometimes a smaller line that finishes off a main stroke of a letter, which is called a serif; and each letter has what is called a main body. The differences in the strokes, the serifs, and the main body are the factors that distinguish one typeface from another. Some letters have strokes of comparatively uniform thickness, while others show extreme contrast between thick and thin strokes. The letters of some typefaces have no serifs at all, and the letters of others have either rounded serifs or pointed serifs or square serifs. Some typefaces have letters that are heavily shaded, and others have letters that are lightly shaded.

Typefaces have been placed in several categories, and it is useful to mention them, though the distinctions are often very fine, and there is a certain amount of overlapping among categories.

One category is designated as old style. Old-style typefaces are characterized by open, wide, round letters, strokes of relatively uniform thickness, and rounded or

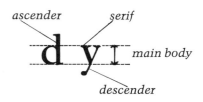

ascender   serif   main body   descender

Garamond
Caslon
Janson

Old-style typefaces

Times Roman

Caledonia

Bodoni
Modern typefaces

Baskerville
Transitional typeface

Clarendon
Square serif

Helvetica
Sans serif

pointed serifs. Examples of old style are Garamond, Caslon, and Janson.

The other major category is called modern (though not what we think of as modern, since it was designed over two hundred years ago). The letters in these typefaces are more mechanically perfect; there is great contrast between thick and thin strokes; the shading is heavy; and the serifs are thin and straight. Examples of modern typefaces include Times Roman, Caledonia, and Bodoni.

In between old style and modern are those typefaces that are called transitional. These are more angular than old style, with sharper contrast between thick and thin strokes. The most widely used of these typefaces is Baskerville.

Finally, there are square serif (or Egyptian) and sans serif (or Gothic). The former, of which Clarendon and Cairo are examples, has square serifs, uniform strokes, and little contrast; the latter, of which Helvetica and News Gothic and Futura are examples, are perfectly plain, with no serifs and strokes of uniform thickness.

The differences in typefaces might be subtle, but the overall effect of the use of one typeface rather than another can be very important, and for this reason the choice of the right typeface for any given book is perhaps the designer's most difficult job. Depending on this choice, the book may have a feeling of lightness or heaviness, of informality or formality.

Once the designer has selected the typeface most

suited to the manuscript, he must concern himself with the size of the type. Type is measured in points, from the top of the ascender to the bottom of the descender, and most types are available in sizes from six points to seventy-two points. However, the most common type sizes for the main text of a book—because they are the most legible—are ten or eleven point. These will not be used for books for young children, or books especially designed for elderly people who may have poor eyesight, both of whom would require larger type, but for the average reader they are the most acceptable sizes.

Type size is also measured by width, but this measurement comes into account at the time the typeface is being chosen. The reason for this is that each single typeface is classified according to character per pica (designated as c.p.p.), which permits the designer to know how many characters of any typeface can fit on one line, depending, of course, on the length of that line. The designer's choice of a typeface, in that case, could be influenced not only by aesthetic reasons, but by the publisher's desire to have a book that seems longer or shorter, whichever the case may be.

In addition to specifying the typeface and its size, as well as the length of the line, the designer must decide on the amount of space he wants between each line. This is called leading; it is measured in points and is determined by the size of the type to be used and the length of the line. The designer will sum up his requirements for the composition of the main text of a

Trump 14 point

Trump 12 point

Trump 10 point

Typeface

Typeface

Typeface

Three examples of fourteen point type

Baskerville
Baskerville Italic

Size	6	7	8	9	10	11	12	14	16
Picas									
10	36	34	32	29	26	24	23	21	17
12	43	41	38	35	31	29	28	25	20
14	50	48	44	41	36	34	32	29	24
16	58	54	50	46	42	38	37	33	27
18	65	61	57	52	47	43	41	37	31
20	72	68	63	58	52	48	46	41	34
22	79	75	69	64	57	53	51	45	38
24	86	82	76	70	62	58	55	49	41
26	94	88	82	75	68	62	60	53	44
28	101	95	88	81	73	67	64	57	48
30	108	102	95	87	78	72	69	62	51

Character per pica chart

book with, for example, the following: Baskerville 10/11 x 23. By this he means he wants 10 point Baskerville, with 1 point of leading, and a line that measures 23 picas.

Example of Baskerville 10/11 x 23

Baskerville, the fine transitional face named for the eighteenth-century English printer, is available in several contemporary versions. The Linotype cutting is most faithful to the original roman and was produced from a complete font cast from the original matrices, exhumed at Paris in 1929.

Aachen Bold

Albertus

Americana

Aster Outline

Blippo Bold

Bodoni Bold

BROADWAY

Bubble Outline

Caslon No. 540

Caslon Extra Bold

Cooper Black

Egyptian

Franklin Gothic

Futura Light

GOLD RUSH

One area in which the designer has great freedom to assert his personal taste is in his design of the title page, part titles, and chapter openings. These often involve the use of what are called display faces—that is, type that is used to display, to call attention through a larger size.

There are a large number of vastly different display types available to the designer, and they come in many sizes. There is no reason for this display type to be of the same typeface as the main body of the text, but it should not, of course, clash with it.

The title page is important: it can, as do the titles preceding a film, set the mood for the entire book. A serious, scholarly work will usually be best presented by a simple title page, soberly stating with dignified type the name of the book, the subtitle if there is one, the name of the author, the name of the publisher, and sometimes the date of first publication.

A children's book, on the other hand, will have a more fanciful title page—or spread of two facing pages—

utilizing large display type and almost always an illustration.

A biography or a work of history will often have a frontispiece—usually a photograph or map relevant to the text—facing the title page. The display face used for the title might attempt to create the period of history covered by the book, just as the typeface used throughout the text of the book will. The same applies to a novel, as well, though novels do not generally have pictorial frontispieces.

The variety of possible title pages is infinite—they can be serious or whimsical, strictly formal, or engagingly informal. Above all, however, they give us the essential information about the book and present this information in a way appropriate to the book's contents.

The designer has choices, too, when it comes to part titles, though usually these will be presented simply—in a type size larger than that used for the main body of the text. When it comes to chapter titles and openings, however, the designer has more scope in which to work.

The chapter title can carry out the spirit of the book, but, first of all, the designer must keep in mind the length of each title. Whether the length of each can be kept to one line, or whether two or even more lines will be needed will help her or him to decide what typeface and size to use. In any case, of course, these titles will be printed in a typeface considerably larger than that used in the text. They will sometimes consist of all capital letters and sometimes capitals and lower case. Most

Helvetica

L&C Hairline

OLD BOWERY

PRISMA

PROFILE

SAPPHIRE

Serif Gothic Bold

Souvenir Light

Tiffany Heavy

TRUMP

Typewriter

Univers 65

Windsor

Various display faces

Title pages from a children's picture book, an adult novel, a nature photography book

chapter titles are simply designed, but from time to time a designer will want to carry out a decorative motif from the title page.

Because the display type used for chapter titles is usually placed lower than the top of the normal type page, the designer must precisely designate the placement of the chapter title. The distance between the top of the page and the chapter title is called the sinkage, and the amount or depth of sinkage is stated in terms of picas.

A few more small decisions must be made by the designer, such as the selection and placing of page numbers or folios, and the design of the running heads. These will be largely dictated by the kind of typeface used in the main body of the text.

Once the designer has decided on the typeface, he or she will prepare a precise castoff, or character count, which gives the number of characters in the manuscript. This is an exacting, but essential, job. Each letter, number, punctuation mark, and space is considered as one unit in this count. The most accurate way of counting the number of units or characters is, naturally, to simply count them one by one. This will give the exact length of the manuscript. Another way, though not as precise, is to count the characters in several lines of the manuscript and thus arrive at an average number of characters per line. Then the average number of lines per page can be calculated, and the number of charac-

Designer's diagram showing placement of running heads, folios, and text

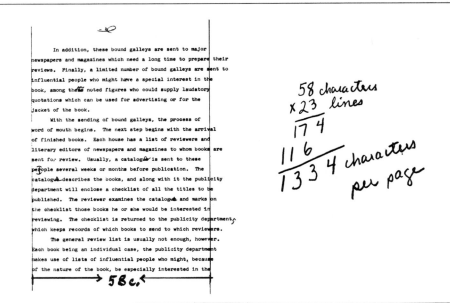

In addition, these bound galleys are sent to major newspapers and magazines which need a long time to prepare their reviews. Finally, a limited number of bound galleys are sent to influential people who might have a special interest in the book, among them noted figures who could supply laudatory quotations which can be used for advertising or for the jacket of the book.

With the sending of bound galleys, the process of word of mouth begins. The next step begins with the arrival of finished books. Each house has a list of reviewers and literary editors of newspapers and magazines to whom books are sent for review. Usually, a catalogue is sent to these people several weeks or months before publication. The catalogue describes the books, and along with it the publicity department will enclose a checklist of all the titles to be published. The reviewer examines the catalogue and marks on the checklist those books he or she would be interested in reviewing. The checklist is returned to the publicity department, which keeps records of which books to send to which reviewers.

The general review list is usually not enough, however. Each book being an individual case, the publicity department makes use of lists of influential people who might, because of the nature of the book, be especially interested in the

*Character count of man-
uscript page*

58 characters
× 23 lines
174
116
1334 characters
per page

ters per line times the number of lines per page will give a fair idea of the number of characters per page. (A well-typed, double-spaced, clean manuscript—the same typewriter used throughout—is a great help in this method.)

Most manuscripts, however, do not contain only straight text, and variants must be carefully considered. There might be extracts—quoted material that is set apart from the main body of the text—as well as notes or poetry, all of which would be set in smaller type and take up less space. On the other hand, there could be part titles, chapter titles, subheads, sub-subheads, all of which would require different type sizes and most probably take up more space. Short lines of dialogue must be considered, and the designer must take into account that the opening page of each chapter will begin several inches from the top of the page. Furthermore, front matter and back matter must be calculated separately, and illustrations must be taken into account when determining the length of the finished book.

At this point, the designer sends a copy of the manuscript to the compositor to have his character count checked and see if the typeface he has chosen will fit the desired number of pages. Each typeface sets differently, and minor adjustments in leading might have to be made.

There are several more decisions a designer must make. One involves the area of the type page—its width and its length. This includes only the area on which the text will be printed and not the margins. This decision is dictated by appearance, economic factors, and readability. The margins are, of course, determined by the size of the type area, the margins being in a sense the frame for the text.

Appearance means, simply, what would look best for a given text, while the economic factor concerns the desired length of the book: the more words per page, the fewer pages required, and thus the less paper required. As for readability, it has been shown that the human eye can most easily span a line that has no more than 65 or 70 characters in it.

The width of the characters of each typeface differs, and a designer designates the width of his line of type in picas. The other common measure in typography is the point, so it is important to keep these measures in mind. There are approximately 72 points to an inch and 12 points to a pica. Thus, a pica equals about one sixth of an inch. The rulers used by designers show picas on one edge and inches on the other.

Once the designer has completed the design, he transmits his plans onto sheets of a special drawing paper. After ruling off the exact size of the trimmed page and of the text area, he shows how the type—both main text and display faces—should be placed within it. All the information necessary for the compositor and printer must be included: the typeface for each part, the size, the leading, and all other specifications.

This layout, which accompanies the manuscript along the various steps of production, will usually include detailed plans for all of the front and back matter; a sample chapter opening; and two facing pages of text with running heads and folios, as well as specifications for special matter such as extracts, footnotes, subheads, and sub-subheads.

Once this layout is completed, the designer marks up the manuscript and gives it to the production department. It is then sent to the compositor who prepares and submits sample pages. When those have been approved, the manuscript can go into production. However, the designer's job is not finished. Often, he or she will consult with the production supervisor concerning the choice of paper; and, in all cases, the designer follows the book along its various stages to see that his

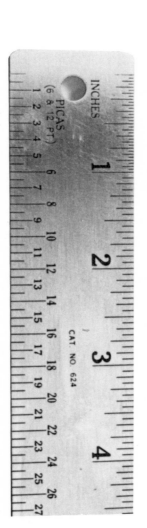

Ruler with pica scale on left edge, inches on right

plans have been faithfully carried out.

In addition, before the book is actually printed, the designer is generally called upon to prepare a mechanical to be used for platemaking. A mechanical is the final assembly of all elements of each page of the book. It is prepared according to indications that show the precise way each page should look; everything that is to go into the book will be shown or indicated on the mechanical. Precision and neatness are essential, since all the elements in their correct positions will be photographed, and the films will serve to make the plates used in printing the book.

The first step in making the mechanical is usually ruling an artboard for page size, trim size, and placement of "bleeding" photographs that will extend to one or more of the trimmed edges of the page. This ruling is done in light blue, a color not picked up by the camera.

This line bleeds off right trim

Reproduction proofs (final, corrected proofs printed on specially treated paper) are cut up and carefully pasted on the board with rubber cement or wax. Running heads and folios, too, are pasted in their correct positions, and extreme care must be taken for spacing and margins.

As for illustrations, line images—which appear in the book as a solid color—can be pasted in with the type copy, but continuous tone or halftone copy, which contains shadings and must first be photographed through a screen, cannot be pasted on the mechanical. Instead, blank spaces, with a key to the illustration that will fill that space on the film, will be left. These halftone il-

COMPOSITION SPECIFICATIONS

To _____ Date _____   Title _Toliver's Secret_

Imprint _CROWN_   Author _EWB_

Prod. Sup. _MW_   Editor _DB_   Designer _BM_

Illustrations: B&W Line _NONE_   B&W Halftone _20 pp_   Color _NONE_

Char. Per Line _50_   Char. Per Page _1350_   Total FM _6 pp_   Total Pages _176 pp_

Lines Per Page _25_   Total Char. _____   Total Text _153 pp_

Trim Size _5½_ x _8¼_ Type Page Size includes r.h. & folio _23_ x _39½_ Picas. Margins: Head _9/16"_ Gutter _3/4"_

Body Matter	Type Face	Size	Sink	Space Ab. & Bel.	Indent
Text	GARAMOND #3	14/17x23	See layout		1 em ¶
Par. Indent					1 em
Left R.H.	GARAMOND #3, SMALL CAPS	12 PT	9/16"		2 ems
Copy	BOOK TITLE				
Right R.H.	NONE				
Copy					
Folios	GARAMOND #3, ITALIC	12 PT			
Ch. Opening Folio	DISPLAY TO COME				
Part No.	—				
Part Title	—				
Chap. No.					
Chap. Title	TO COME				
Sub Title	NONE				
Opening Style	REG 1 EM ¶ INDENT				
Extract	NONE				
Captions	NONE				
Poetry	"				
Footnotes	"				
Index	"				
Glossary	"				
Bibliography	"				

Composition order

Set text: 14/17x23 pi Garamond #3, O.S. figures, 1 em ¶ indents throughout

Do not close lines

8E

Toliver's Secret ①

A — Set chpt nos. throughout as tagline

I

one em ¶ indent throughout → ☐ Grandfather must have lost his wits.

→ ☐ Ellen was sure her grandfather had lost his wits when she saw
him slip into the dark kitchen and lock the door with a big key. Without giving his usual cheery greeting he tiptoed to the window and
pinned the heavy curtains together with a knitting needle.

    "Don't want anyone peeping in this morning," he said to Ellen's
mother who was making bread on a table by the fireplace.

    Lights from a small fire on the hearth darted about the big old
kitchen. From the dark corner where she sat brushing her hair, Ellen
could see light glimmering on a tiny silver box he carried in his
hand.

    "Is the loaf ready now?" Grandfather whispered to her mother.

*Manuscript page showing
designer's specifications*

the big old kitchen. From the dark corner where she sat brushing her hair, Ellen could see light glimmering on a tiny silver box he carried in his hand.

"Is the loaf ready now?" Grandfather whispered to her mother.

Mother's white cap fluttered up and down, but she did not speak. Very carefully she patted and shaped a small round loaf of bread.

"Well, then, let us go ahead," Grandfather said as he gingerly placed the silver box on top of the lump of dough.

Ellen stared at the little box. It was his favorite silver snuffbox. She was too surprised to speak when she saw him press the snuffbox into the dough, smooth over the hole that he had made and dust off his hands. His round face had a wide impish smile.

"No one will find it there," he said gleefully. He stepped back and cocked his head to one side. "Bake it crisp and brown, Abby, with a good strong crust. It has a long way to travel."

"You're quite sure no one will find it, Father?" Mother sounded frightened.

"Now don't worry, Abby. No one will find it." He patted her shoulder and gave her a kiss.

Ellen saw that he was wearing the white wig with

100

the turned-up tail that he always wore when he went to the tavern. Underneath his blue wool coat he wore a long waistcoat with brass buttons down the front. He was short and stout and the buttons marched down his waistcoat in an outward curve. He never wore these clothes when he worked in his barbershop.

Ellen was so puzzled she had to speak up. "Whatever are you planning to do, Grandfather?"

Quickly her grandfather spun around and peered into the deep shadows of the old kitchen. He gave a sharp cry that made her jump up. "I thought you had gone to the corner pump, Ellie!"

Ellen curtsied. "I was just about to make the bed, but I'll leave now, Grandfather." She picked up her red cloak and pulled the hood over her long brown hair.

Grandfather stepped across the room and grasped her by the shoulders. "Don't ever speak of what you have seen, Ellen Toliver," he warned in a gruff voice she had never heard him use before. He was usually so friendly and cheerful, even in the early morning, even with the British officers around. But now his twinkling blue eyes looked as hard as points of steel. Ellen was so startled she dropped her cloak.

"But I was just wondering—"

101

Sample pages marked for corrections

---

the big old kitchen. From the dark corner where she sat brushing her hair, Ellen could see light glimmering on a tiny silver box he carried in his hand.

"Is the loaf ready now?" Grandfather whispered to her mother.

Mother's white cap fluttered up and down, but she did not speak. Very carefully she patted and shaped a small round loaf of bread.

"Well, then, let us go ahead," Grandfather said as he gingerly placed the silver box on top of the lump of dough.

Ellen stared at the little box. It was his favorite silver snuffbox. She was too surprised to speak when she saw him press the snuffbox into the dough, smooth over the hole that he had made and dust off his hands. His round face had a wide impish smile.

"No one will find it there," he said gleefully. He stepped back and cocked his head to one side. "Bake it crisp and brown, Abby, with a good strong crust. It has a long way to travel."

"You're quite sure no one will find it, Father?" Mother sounded frightened.

"Now don't worry, Abby. No one will find it." He patted her shoulder and gave her a kiss.

Ellen saw that he was wearing the white wig with

100

the turned-up tail that he always wore when he went to the tavern. Underneath his blue wool coat he wore a long waistcoat with brass buttons down the front. He was short and stout and the buttons marched down his waistcoat in an outward curve. He never wore these clothes when he worked in his barbershop.

Ellen was so puzzled she had to speak up. "Whatever are you planning to do, Grandfather?"

Quickly her grandfather spun around and peered into the deep shadows of the old kitchen. He gave a sharp cry that made her jump up. "I thought you had gone to the corner pump, Ellie!"

Ellen curtsied. "I was just about to make the bed, but I'll leave now, Grandfather." She picked up her red cloak and pulled the hood over her long brown hair.

Grandfather stepped across the room and grasped her by the shoulders. "Don't ever speak of what you have seen, Ellen Toliver," he warned in a gruff voice she had never heard him use before. He was usually so friendly and cheerful, even in the early morning, even with the British officers around. But now his twinkling blue eyes looked as hard as points of steel. Ellen was so startled she dropped her cloak.

"But I was just wondering—"

101

Final mechanical

lustrations are inserted after a film has been made of the mechanical.

A designer's job requires creative as well as technical skills, to say nothing of a great deal of hard work. It is rewarding work, however, since good design can contribute considerably to the success of a book.

The Jacket Designer

Largely because of its effectiveness in selling a book, great importance is placed on the design of the book jacket. Originally, the jacket—a heavier than usual paper wrapped around the book—served largely as protection against dirt, dust, and grease. Today, the jacket has another, more important function. More than a protective wrapper, it is used to attract readers and to identify the book, both by its graphic design and by what is written on it. It is, in a sense, an advertisement for the book as well as a quick source of information about it. For these reasons, great attention must be paid not only to the artwork to be used on a jacket, but to the written information that is printed on it.

A successful book jacket is eye-catching and informative. It must, first of all, attract the professional book buyer, that is, the bookstore owner who usually sees the jacket long before he or she sees the book and stocks copies of the book on the basis of its jacket as well as the salesman's presentation. Next, the jacket must catch the eye of customers browsing through a bookstore. Many potential readers, looking for a book to read or to give, will be drawn to a book on display by its jacket—passing by the books with nondescript jackets for those with attractive ones. They will then read what is written on the jacket flaps and, on the basis of that, will then make their decision, sometimes skimming through the book itself before doing so. Another factor that might be kept in mind when a jacket is designed is whether or not it will photograph well, for a photo could be useful for a catalog or for advertising. Many books become known through eye-catching jackets that "identify" them for the reader.

The designer of the jacket is generally chosen by the publishing house's art director, who has a good idea of the kind of jacket wanted. With this in mind, he or she will give the assignment on the basis of a jacket designer's past work, which will have shown a style that seems best suited to the book in question. Is the jacket designer most comfortable with illustrations, which might be done by another artist, or with photographs, or is he or she especially imaginative in the use of type?

The conception of the book jacket necessarily takes a longer time than the actual execution because it is the conception that involves a creative act, one requiring thought, imagination, flair, and a sympathetic understanding of the book, while the actual execution is

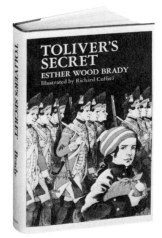

children's novel

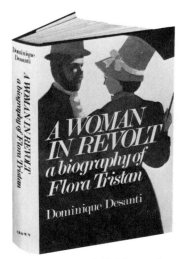

adult biography

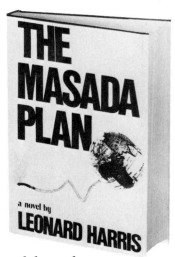

adult novel

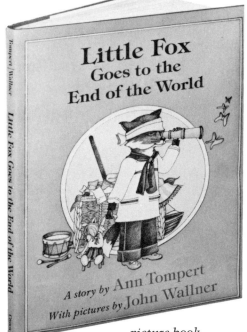

picture book

Book Jackets

art book

Jacket spine

largely a matter of mechanical skill, though this skill might be of great importance if a complicated illustration is involved. Preparation of the jacket mechanical is as complex and demanding as that of any book illustration.

At the very beginning, the jacket designer will discuss the job with the art director. The latter will have an idea of the kind of jacket wanted and will know the budget for the jacket—the amount of money that can be spent will determine the number of colors that the designer will be allowed to use. Following that, a conference with the editor of the book may be useful to the designer as will, of course, a reading of the manuscript.

Furthermore, the designer will need to be told exactly what written matter, or copy, will be placed on the jacket. The front of the jacket will certainly contain the title of the book and the name of the author. The length of the title and the length of the author's name will necessarily influence the choice of type. A quote from a well-known critic, or a line such as "by the author of...," which will then mention the title of an earlier successful book by the same author, could be included to identify the author whose name might be less well known than that of his previous book.

On the spine of the jacket, the designer will work out the placement of the title of the book, the author, and the name of the publishing house. This is important because the book might be displayed on a bookshelf where only the spine would show rather than on a table or in a

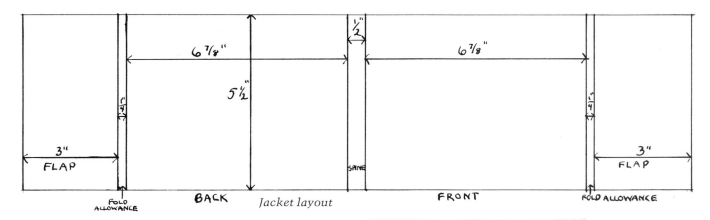

Jacket layout

Artist's jacket sketch (with type)

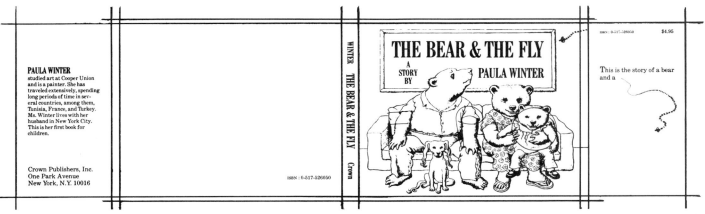

Jacket mechanical

window where the front of the jacket would be showing.

The back of the jacket might have written material—
descriptive of the book, or biographical information
about the author—or a photograph of the author, or
merely decorative matter. The two flaps, the ends of the
jacket, which fold inside the front and back covers of
the volume, will generally show the price and give information about the contents of the book and/or about
the author. All this written material is called the blurb.

If the editor of the book feels that the author's name
is of special importance, he must tell this to the designer; if, instead, the title of the book should be em-
phasized, the designer must be thus informed. In other
words, before beginning his task, the jacket designer
must have every possible piece of information that will
help him create a successful book jacket.

Once he or she has all this information, it is time to
begin thinking about the jacket. All we have to do to
see the infinite variety of book jackets possible is to
spend a short time in a bookstore or in a library looking
at books. Each designer has had to face the same problem of creating a jacket that is both faithful to the content of the book and will attract the reader's attention.
The solutions are endless. There are jackets that use
type alone—and the different kinds of type available for
display are very many, to say nothing of hand lettering
designed for a specific jacket. Photos are used, collages,
montages, drawings, paintings, decorative pat-

terns....Jackets can be stark; they can be florid; they can be dramatic or humorous, directly informative or strongly evocative.

Faced with all these choices, but limited by the budget and the nature of the book, the designer must find what he feels is the best approach, the one that will satisfy the needs of the book and the taste of the public.

Several solutions could come to mind, in which case the designer should make sketches of what he feels are the best of his ideas. He then brings these sketches to the publishing house, where his ideas are debated among the staff. The art director, of course, will have his say. The editor, too, is bound to have strong feelings and probably suggestions. However, perhaps the decisive opinion will come from the sales department, since the jacket's primary function is to sell books. The jacket is generally the salesman's only visual tool in selling a book to a bookseller; he cannot possibly carry copies of each book that he is selling, so—except in cases where the appearance of the book is of great importance—he will sell instead on the strength of the jacket or a proof of that jacket. The look of that jacket is of great importance—almost equal to that of the advertising budget or promotion plans when the salesman tries to place the largest number of copies of a book in the stores.

Because he is better acquainted with bookselling than are most other members of the publishing house, because he is closer to the marketplace, the salesman's

opinions should be carefully considered. It is not unusual that a jacket, though enthusiastically accepted by
the art and editorial departments, is rejected by the
sales department, on commercial grounds. There is, of
course, no reason for a jacket to be in poor taste or un-
faithful to the contents of the book. Yet, the book jacket
has become a sales tool, and as such its commercial
value is of prime importance.

From the number of sketches submitted, one will
prove most acceptable to the art, editorial, and sales departments. Members of each department may well have
suggestions for improvements, but, with all of these in
mind, the jacket designer will know exactly how he
must proceed. He can begin work on the mechanical for
the jacket—that is, he will execute the design from
which the final jacket will be printed. This is precision
work, and it is essential that he know the exact format
of the book as well as its bulk, so that the jacket will—as
it must—fit comfortably around the finished book. Once
the mechanical is completed, the jacket is ready for
printing. (The actual printing of a jacket will be discussed in the chapter on the color printer.)

No one can say whether a jacket is good or bad. There
are aesthetic judgments, and these are of some value.
But many people in publishing say that the successful
jacket is the one that has been wrapped around the book
that sells. This is a cynical attitude, but perhaps it is
the most realistic of all.

The Production Supervisor

Modern technology has advanced so rapidly in recent years that methods of book production today differ radically from those of just a few decades ago; by the same token, today's methods will most likely be altered and even outdated a few years from now. Nonetheless, the goal of book production remains and will remain the same: to transform a manuscript into a printed and bound book within a specific budget.

The person responsible for planning and keeping track of that transformation is the production supervisor. This man or woman must keep up with technological advances and have a solid background in all phases of book production. It is essential, too, for the production supervisor to know the advantages and the shortcomings of the available suppliers, for it is his or her job to select the compositor, the printer, and the binder, and to choose the paper to be used for each book, as well as the cloth to be used for the case of each book. Since several books will be in production at the same time—and at different stages—the job is a complicated one, involving not only the selection of each supplier and the control of the supplier's materials or work, but also coordinating the work and schedules of a large number of suppliers and craftsmen.

The production supervisor, too, acts as a liaison between the publishing house and the various suppliers. He or she can advise an editor, in the preliminary stages, as to the possibility or the impossibility of doing a certain book at a reasonable price. There are times when an editor would like to go ahead with a project, but feels it would cost too much to do so because of production problems; consultation with the production supervisor could prove the editor wrong, since the former might be aware of new equipment or alternate methods of printing a book that would enable it to be produced in the right way and at an economical price.

It is most important for the production supervisor to keep in mind the possible conflict between budget restrictions and the quality desired. He or she will most likely know where to go for the best possible printing and binding, but that knowledge is not enough; the production supervisor's job is not only to have the job done well, but to have it done within the limitations of the budget for any given book. The printer, or binder, who might do the finest job, could be too expensive, so the production supervisor must be in touch with other, less expensive printers or binders who can do an acceptable job if carefully checked and supervised. For each solution, there must be an alternate.

It is essential that the production supervisor be on good working terms with a number of suppliers and know which would be best suited for each book. Several factors are involved in this choice. Knowledge of each supplier's equipment is essential in determining that supplier's capability to do a given job. The supplier's reliability in maintaining a high quality of work is vital, as is the supplier's reliability when it comes to keeping to a schedule. The production supervisor must know which supplier will be available at which time and which will understand the needs of the publisher—just as the publisher's production supervisor will have to know the possibilities and limitations of the printers and binders involved in any project.

Quality is, obviously, of great importance, but one of the first tasks of the production supervisor, after receiving the manuscript, is to obtain cost estimates from several different suppliers. Selection of a supplier depends on the above-mentioned factors, but it also depends on cost. Since different suppliers charge different amounts for their work, these estimates will usually have to be obtained from several suppliers before a decision can be made.

Book publishers work on a very small margin of profit, and for this reason it is most important that the publisher know just how much each book will cost. A

```
We are pleased to quote on your 4/c process insert based on the
following specifications:

Trim Size:           ·  8 x 9

Pages:                  Sixteen

Quantity:               6,000 / 10,000

Copy:                   4 Drop out half tones we to shoot black &
                        white reproduction; balance of material as
                        paged negatives for B & W and 4/c process.
                        There are to be 6 pages in 4/c process.

Paper:                  Crown to supply 70# smooth offset.
6,000 copies                                     10,000 copies
8,000 sheets 23 x 35                             12,000 sheets 23 x 35
Prices:
6,000                                            10,000
Plates:  $200.00                                 Plates: $ 200.00
Press:    900.00                                 Press:   1200.00
*Prep:    300.00                                 Prep:     300.00
*Color                                           Color
Key:      120.00                                 Key:      120.00
         _____                                        _____
         15.20.00                                        1820.00

* Note:  Prep price is a approx. figure.
         Color Key only if desired.
```

Estimate quotation from printer

publisher sells most of his books at 60 percent of their retail price; 10 percent of that retail price is paid to the author; and there are other expenses such as overhead (which includes salaries, rent, telephone, warehouse costs, and office supplies), publicity, advertising, and so on. The cost of the actual production of the book will be at least 20 percent of the retail price, so there remains very little, if any, profit on a book that sells only moderately well. Obviously, then, an error in a production estimate can be financially disastrous; a miscalculation, an added expense, or a forgotten detail can easily mean the difference between profit and loss on any one title.

This cost estimate must take into account every facet of production. It is divided into two main parts: plant costs and manufacturing costs. The former are costs that occur only once, no matter how many copies of the book are printed. These plant costs include composition—the setting of all type both in the book and on the jacket, proofs, mechanicals, and artwork for the book and jacket, plates, and binding dies. The more copies of each title printed, the lower the cost of these items per copy, since these nonrecurring costs will thus be divided by a larger figure.

Manufacturing costs, on the other hand, are those that depend on the number of copies of each book that are printed and bound. These include paper, binding, and presswork—though printing a larger quantity at one time will reduce the cost of the latter since preparation of the presses is required only at the beginning of a run.

As we learn more about the processes of book man-ufacturing, we will become aware of the vast number of details to be taken into account along the way. With so many details, it is necessary for the production super-visor and his or her assistants to set up schedules and maintain records—of when things should be done, and when things are actually done. This is important for many reasons.

A great deal of planning, in each department of the publishing house, goes into the publication of a book, from the moment that the manuscript is ready. For sales and publicity purposes, dates on which proofs and finished books will be ready must be determined far in advance. Delays can be costly, can mean fewer sales,

<u>Four</u> <u>Color</u> <u>Picture</u> <u>Book</u>

$6.95 list price   32 pages   8 x 10   10,000 edition

Preseparated artwork

Royalty 10% of list price (.695 rounded off to .70)

$3.75 net to publisher/ 46% off list price

<u>COSTS</u>		<u>OVERHEAD</u>	
Printing	.15	Editorial & Production	.22
Paper	.10	Advertising & Promotion	.30
Jacket	.06	Cost of Selling	.30
Binding	.75	Shipping & Warehouse	.22
Preparation:		General Administrative	.46
Type	.02		
Plates	.02	TOTAL OVERHEAD	1.50
General	.30	(Total Overhead 40% of Net)	
Jacket	.02		
TOTAL	1.42		

Total	1.42	Net	3.75
Total Overhead	1.50	Total Expenses	3.62
Royalty	.70		
TOTAL EXPENSES	3.62	PROFIT	.13
		(Profit 3½% of Net)	

Publisher's complete estimate for four color picture book

and can undermine carefully prepared publicity campaigns. Yet, with so many steps involved, and so many different suppliers and people involved, delays are difficult to avoid. The failure—and it can be a perfectly understandable one—of one person, one process, or of one company along the line can cause a change in the entire schedule and consequently a delay of weeks or even months in the publication of a book.

In spite of possible delays, however, it is essential that some kind of schedule be set up by the production supervisor, and that every effort be made to keep to it. This schedule must take into consideration time for composition, proofreading of galleys, page makeup, reading of page proofs, preparation of an index, further corrections, and platemaking, printing, and binding. In all, a publisher must plan on four to five months for the manufacture of a book. There can be exceptions, jobs that can be rushed through in as short a time as a few weeks, if necessary, but these are not common.

In addition to obtaining estimates, choosing suppliers, setting up schedules, and keeping up with each step of the book's production, the production supervisor is the person who will—sometimes with the help of the designer—choose the paper to be used. The selection of paper is a crucial one, since paper is not only important for the appearance of the book, but also represents a considerable percentage of the costs of making a book. Though the advice of the paper salesman and the printer can be invaluable to the production

PRODUCTION SCHEDULE
#1

TITLE: BOOKS: FROM WRITER TO READER   CC: Publicity
PROJECTED # PAGES: 208 + 16   Inventory Control
TRIM SIZE: 8" x 9"   Copyediting
BOOKS WANTED: August, 1976   Marketing
PUBLICATION DATE: October, 1976   Sales Department

Ms. in Production   2/6

Design to Edit. for O.K.   2/19   (2 wks.)

Design O.K.   2/20   (1 day)   REMARKS

Ms. to Comp.   2/20   Jacket flap copy due

Sample PP. from Comp.   2/26   (4 dys.)   June 4.

Sample PP. O.K.   2/27   (1 day)   _____

GG. to Edit. from Comp.   3/18   (3 wks.)   _____

GG. ret'd. to Comp.   4/23   (2 wks.)   _____

PP. to Edit. from Comp.   5/7   (2 wks.)   _____

PP. ret'd. to Comp.   5/21   (2 wks.)

Repro from Comp.   5/28   (1 wk.)

Repro/Mech. from Designer   6/11   (2 wks.)

    BM. & Index Ms. to Comp.   5/28   (3 wks. from pp.)

    BM. & Index GG. to Edit.   6/4   (4 dys.)

    BM. & Index GG. ret'd. to Comp. 6/8   (2 dys.)

    BM. & Index PP. to Edit.   6/14   (4 dys.)

    BM. & Index PP. ret'd. to Comp. 6/16   (2 dys.)

    BM. & Index Repro   6/21   (3 dys.)

Copy to Printer   6/11-6/23 (Index)

Book Blues Due   7/2   (3 wks.)

Book Blues O.K.   7/4   (2 dys.)

Off Press   7/16   (1½ wks.)

Bound Book Due   wk. of 8/6 (3 wks.)

supervisor when he or she buys paper, it is most useful for the latter to bring a knowledge and understanding of the various qualities of paper to his or her job.

Several factors are involved in the selection of paper. Color is one. Though at a casual glance all paper might seem white to us, its range in color is actually considerable: from a pure white to a rather yellowish white.

Another factor is opacity, the amount of light that will show through from one side of the page to the other side. Some papers can be seen through rather easily, while others are completely impenetrable.

Another important distinction in paper is its finish, or smoothness. Papers vary from what is called rough, or antique, finish—most commonly used for books—to glossy, which is used for halftone illustrations.

Weight, too, is indicated in the choice of paper, as is bulk, which has nothing to do with weight. Bulk is important, since it determines the thickness of the book, and a thick book is often desirable for commercial reasons since it can make a short book seem longer than it actually is.

The final factor in the selection of paper is price. Prices of paper vary considerably, and the selection of paper might well depend on the overall budget for the book. Buying large quantities of paper at one time—for use in several books—can constitute a saving, and for this reason the production supervisor should take this into consideration in planning for the publisher's entire list.

IMPOSITION

Title of Book:..

Publisher:...

Paper: Size, weight and finish: Trim size: .... x ....   Rough Trim: ....   Smooth Trim: ....

.... x .... — /500 — ....

Number of pages for which this imposition is to be used:...

To.. ....   **Date**..

QUAD INSERT SHEETWISE

Press Side Guide and Folder Guide

Press Gripper

Front of sheet   *Back of sheet*

The production supervisor's job does not merely involve schedules, estimates, and the selection of suppliers. The members of the production department must carefully follow each step of the book's manufacture and perform various technical functions as well. Important among these is working out what is called the imposition, a diagram of the front and back of the sheet of paper to be used, which shows the printer in what sequence the pages must be arranged so that they will be in the proper order when they are folded for binding. In order to do this, the production supervisor must consult with the printer and the binder, for there are many different kinds of equipment that would determine this imposition, and each printer and binder has his own.

The job of the production supervisor is one of great responsibility. Obviously, it is most important that each book be well produced, for a predetermined cost and within a given period of time.

The Compositor

The first step in the actual production is composition: that is, the mechanical means of changing a manuscript into type or a photographic image that can be used either directly for printing or in the manufacture of printing plates. After nearly a century of relatively little change in methods of composition, the period since the end of World War II has seen rapid advancements that will undoubtedly lead to even more revolutionary developments in the near future, especially in the area of phototypesetting.

The methods of book composition are basically three: hot type, or cast metal; typewriter or direct impression; and phototypesetting. The first of these includes hand composition, Linotype or Intertype, Monotype, and Ludlow.

In the earliest days of printing—back to the time of Gutenberg in 1450—type was set by hand. Because it is both slow and expensive, hand setting is rarely used today for books, and, when it is, it is to set large display type. Nonetheless, many of the problems and principles involved apply to other, more commonly used methods.

The compositor takes the individual metal characters from a type case and puts them in a small metal tray—called a composing stick—which he holds in one hand. This stick is about ten picas deep and has an adjustable bracket which controls the length of the line. Since the lines must be justified—that is, they must come out to an even length—there are thin pieces of metal of varying widths which are placed between each word. When the stick is full, the type is transferred to an oblong metal tray, called a galley, where all the lines are assembled. Spacing between the lines is achieved by the insertion of metal strips, or slugs.

Machine composition was first used in the last part of the nineteenth century with the introduction of the Linotype machine. Linotype was the first and is still the most widely used form of machine composition. (Intertype, too, is much used and is practically identical to Linotype.)

The machine itself is large and complex. An operator sits before a typewriterlike keyboard, the manuscript—which he has studied for any special problems—by his side. When he touches a key representing a letter, number, or punctuation mark, a matrix or mold, held in a metal box called a magazine, above the keyboard, drops through a channel into position in the line being

Pieces of metal type

A composing stick

Type case

Compositor setting type

set. At the end of each word, a space bar is pushed, and an expandable steel wedge–a spaceband–drops into place. When the line is nearly full, the compositor pushes a bar that moves all the spacebands at once, thereby spreading the line as evenly as possible to the desired length. This is possible because the expandable band is thinner at the top and grows gradually thicker at the bottom. When the line is justified in this way, it is moved into a position where molten type metal is forced against it, filling in the incised areas, and a complete line of type, or slug, is produced and ejected onto a galley. The original matrices are then returned to the channels from which they came so that they may be used again.

Each matrix generally contains two characters–roman and italic. Small caps are from a third category and are usually under the roman and italic characters and have no italic form or punctuation marks and figures. Since the Linotype operator must change magazines when he changes typeface or type size, any complications in the copy will cause extra expense. In Linotype, too, the change in any part of a line means resetting the whole line.

This is not true in the case of another form of hot-type composition called Monotype, also developed in the latter part of the nineteenth century. This system makes use of two separate machines: a keyboard and a composing or casting machine. The operator uses the keyboard as if it were a typewriter, but instead of pro-

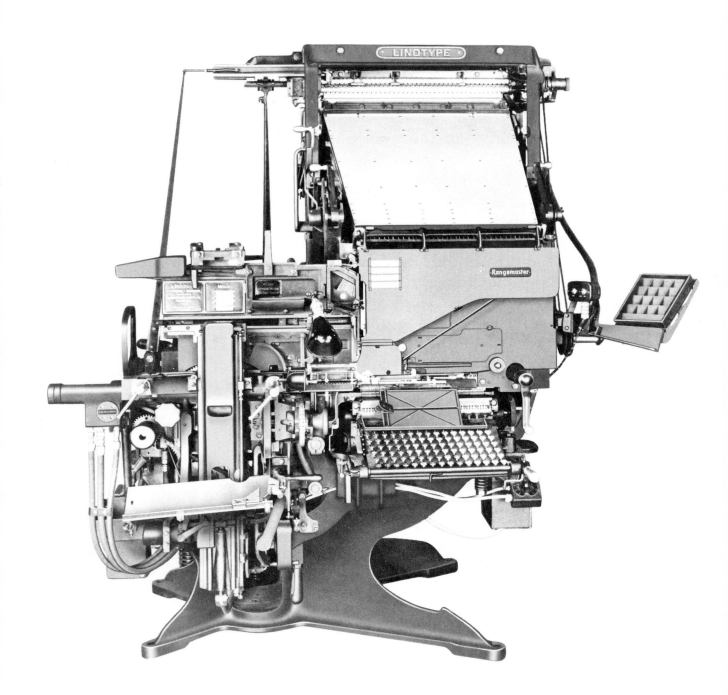

A Linotype machine

ducing readable copy, it produces, by means of compressed air, a roll of perforated ribbon—much like that used in a player piano. This roll, with its perforation or code, is then placed on the machine which follows its coded instructions, casting not a full line like Linotype, but one character at a time. In other words, it chooses, from a matrix case, the mold of the desired letter or figure or punctuation mark and initiates the process of forcing hot metal onto this mold. The result of this is a piece of type that joins other individual characters to form a line of separate pieces of type from which to print or make plates.

Lines are justified automatically at the time of the keyboard operation. When the line is nearly full, a bell rings and the operator pushes various keys to learn exactly how much space must be added to fill out the line to its required length. A button is then pushed, and word spaces are automatically interspersed evenly among the words. When the line is completed, it is ejected onto a galley tray.

Monotype is used largely for complicated setting jobs, because it reproduces individual characters rather than lines and thus allows for greater flexibility. Because more matrices are available, mixing typefaces is easier than with Linotype. Monotype machines also cast longer lines and use a harder metal in casting, which makes for more durable type. Corrections, too, can be made by hand, one letter—rather than one line—at a time, which means less resetting.

Linotype slugs

In spite of these advantages, Monotype remains slower and more costly than Linotype. For these reasons, its use today is limited.

The last form of hot-type composition is called Ludlow, and it too is not often used. Ludlow combines hand and machine operations, the matrices being assembled by hand and locked in a frame similar to a composing stick. This frame is placed over a slot in a casting machine, and hot metal is pressed against the matrices, thereby casting a slug. Ludlow is used for large display type; in book production it is particularly useful for setting recurring running heads, since as many lines as needed can be cast from just one slug.

The second general method of composition, typewriter or direct impression (or sometimes cold type to differentiate it from hot type) is usually adopted as an economy measure. It was developed in the middle of this century, and the theory behind it is that of the ordinary typewriter, though an ordinary typewriter would not give satisfactory enough results to allow its use.

There is no casting of metal type, merely the striking of keys that impress, through high-quality carbon paper, an imprint of a character on a sheet of paper. A printing plate may be made by merely photographing that paper. This method of composition was developed in response to the increased use of a printing method called offset lithography, which requires high-quality proofs—called reproduction proofs—to serve as camera copy. While these repros can be made from hot-metal type, the use

IBM Selectric Composer

of direct impression composition eliminates this intermediate step of proofmaking by producing the camera copy directly.

There are other ways of economizing through the use of typewriter composition. The machines are really finely constructed variations of the typewriter, among them the IBM Executive, the Varityper, and the Composaline and cost far less than does Monotype or Linotype. They take up less space, and they can be operated by men and women who are far less skilled than Linotype or Monotype operators and so are paid less. Too, the operator readily sees mistakes without the aid of proofs and can therefore correct them easily.

The entire procedure is a relatively simple one, yet its disadvantages outweigh its advantages in commercial book production. Justification, considered important for most books, is difficult, and expensive special equipment is required. Proofs, too, are a problem, since only one or two sets of carbons—to serve as proofs—can be obtained, and any extra proofs, which are often essential, can be very costly. The number of fonts available is limited, which restricts the possibility of imaginative design. However, the greatest disadvantage lies in the generally lower quality that results from direct impression. It is impossible for the image to be as sharp as that of hot type—the same characters are being used several times—and the limitations of the machines make uniformity of impression impossible.

The most important change in method of composition in recent years involves phototypesetting. This procedure, as its name implies, is based on the principles of photography.

A large number of different kinds of phototypesetting machines are already in use, and undoubtedly many more and improved ones will be developed. It is difficult to classify these machines, but they all have four basic elements in common: a source of light, a character image, an optical system, and a photo- or light-sensitive material, which can be either film or photographic paper.

It is the light, which flashes at greater or lesser speeds depending on the machine, that projects the character image. A negative, held in either a glass or plastic matrix in a film strip, a drum, a grid, or a disc, generally moves into position according to the coding on a magnetic or perforated tape, or sometimes by the direct instruction of the keyboard operator—depending on the system used.

Because this is a projected image, it arrives from the matrix to the film or light-sensitive paper through a very complicated optical system, which also differs according to the machine used. This optical system is generally composed of lenses of different types and of a reflecting mechanism, such as a prism or a mirror. Through the use of various lenses, it is often possible to project the image—that is, the character—to any desired size.

Finally, the developed film, either positive or negative, can be exposed directly onto a photomechanical plate for printing, or a positive image can be produced on specially treated paper.

As in previously discussed methods of composition, phototypesetting is initiated by a keyboard operator. This compositor can either operate the photographic element directly—projecting the image rather than casting the metal slug—or indirectly by producing the tape that will in turn give instructions to the machine.

Progress is constantly being made in this area of book production, and computers are rapidly coming into use in composition. One of the latest developments is the use of a device that scans the material to be reproduced and breaks up the image electronically into many tiny dots or lines which are so close together that the optical effect is that of a solid character. This image is then

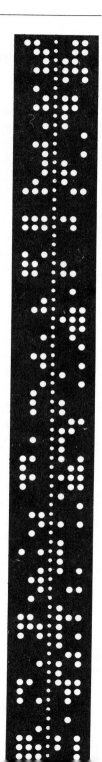

Perforated tape

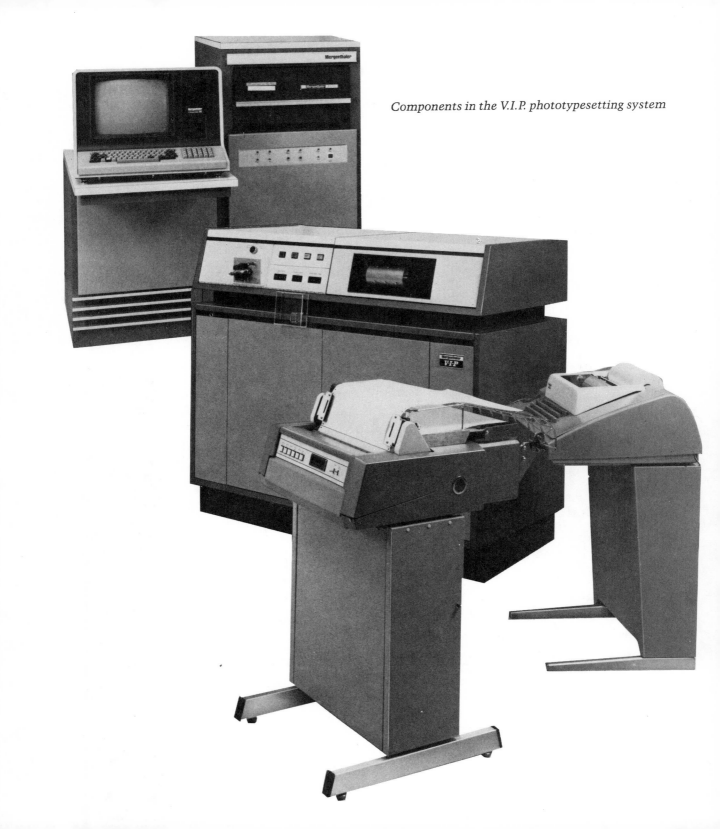

Components in the V.I.P. phototypesetting system

transmitted from the tube to the photographic material.

More and more efficient and economical machines will undoubtedly be developed in the next years, and the publisher will have to decide what method of composition he wishes to use on just that basis: efficiency and economy. Phototypesetting has disadvantages, especially the high cost of corrections and page makeup, as we will see. It has many advantages, too, many of them based on the increased use of offset printing which employs photographic techniques and so has an affinity with phototypesetting.

This new procedure is more flexible and far faster than other methods of composition. The quality of work is generally higher, and phototypesetting will give a sharper image than the best of reproduction proofs, the need for which is eliminated as are the camera stages in platemaking for offset or gravure. Through the lenses, type can be enlarged or reduced to any size. This lessens the amount of storage space necessary in a plant. Light film, too, is obviously easier to handle than is heavy metal used in hot-type composition.

The initial financial investment in phototypesetting—and especially computerized phototypesetting—is high. Yet in the long run, and with increased use, the saving in both time and money will be such that computerized phototypesetting will be the most common, if not the only, means of setting type.

Once the type has been set, by whatever means, it is necessary to check the accuracy of the composition—

that is, to see that it corresponds exactly to the original manuscript; to make certain that the compositor has followed the author's copy, along with the editors' changes, and the designer's instructions. For this purpose, it is necessary to make—or pull—proofs, which are called galley proofs (even in the case of cold-type composition where no galleys are actually involved).

They are called galley proofs because the type in Linotype or Monotype composition is kept in a galley—a shallow metal tray—after it has been set. This tray is usually about twenty-four inches long, corresponding to roughly two to three pages of a book. This type, held tightly in the galley by wooden wedges, is placed on the flatbed of a press. It is inked by a roller, known as a

Galley proof (left) and type in galley tray on flatbed of proof press (right)

A proof press

brayer, and a long sheet of paper is placed over it. An impression is then made by a cylinder which transfers the type image to the paper. There are different kinds of proof presses—some hand-operated and some power-operated, some with a moving bed and some with a stationary bed—but they are all relatively simple machines when compared to a regular printing press, and each has the essential elements of a flatbed, an inking unit, and an impression cylinder.

Cold-type proofs are necessarily different, since no standing type is involved. The typewriter and direct impression machines produce what amounts to one or two carbon copies; phototypesetting machines produce positive photographic prints on paper. Usually more sets of proofs are required than can be made by these

---

AUTHOR'S PROOF

Monotype Composition Co.

Check over carefully. Mark any corrections or changes legibly in margin of proof.

READ BY _____

OK'd By _____

70——Reed——Witness To Revolution——MCC   565

---

soldiers came over to the grave. They took off their hats and spoke very reverently: "What a good fellow he was!" said one. "He came all the way across the world for us. He was one of ours . . ."

Louise lived for another sixteen years. In 1923, in Paris, she married William Bullitt, a former Washington correspondent and later a member of the State Department and the first American Ambassador to the Soviet Union. Louise and Bullitt had a daughter, but the marriage was unhappy and ended in divorce three years later with Bullitt retaining custody of the child. Louise returned to New York where she lived in the same Village apartment she had once shared with Reed at 1 Patchin Place. But the past could not be recaptured so easily. She fled back to Europe again where she died in Paris, of a cerebral hemorrhage, in 1936. She never truly recovered from her loss, as Art Young revealed in his autobiography:

Poor Louise committed slow suicide—went the sad road of narcotic escape. Only a few weeks before she died she sent me a postcard from her Paris studio at 50 rue Vavin.

"I suppose in the end life gets all of us," she wrote. "It nearly has got me now—getting myself and my friends out of jail—living under curious conditions—but never minding much. . . . Know always I send my love to you across the stars. If you get there before I do—or later—tell Jack Reed I love him.

Louise's loss had been painfully personal, but there were also countless numbers of people all over the world who had never known Reed but who had admired and respected him. When the news of his death had first reached America, thousands of jailed radical workers had received it in tragic silence. The press in the United States, which had been quick to revile him during his lifetime, had

---

I do not remember the speeches. I remember more the broken notes of the speakers' voices. I was aware that after a long time they ceased and the banners began to dip back and forth in salute. I heard the first shovel of earth go rolling down and then something snapped in my brain. . . . After an eternity I woke up in my own bed.

But I have been in the Red Square since then—since that day all those people came to bury in all honor our dear Jack Reed. I have been there in the busy afternoon when all Russia hurries by, horses and sleighs and bells and peasants carrying bundles, soldiers singing on their way to the front. Once some of the soldiers came over to the grave. They took off their hats and spoke very reverently: "What a good fellow he was!" said one. "He came all the way across the world for us. He was one of ours . . ."

Louise lived for another sixteen years. In 1923, in Paris, she married William Bullitt, a former Washington correspondent and later a member of the State Department and the first American Ambassador to the Soviet Union. Louise and Bullitt had a daughter, but the marriage was unhappy and ended in divorce seven years later with Bullitt retaining custody of the child. Louise returned to New York where she lived in the same Village apartment she had once shared with Reed at

216

Galley proof marked for correction (left), and corrected page proof (right)

machines, so other processes, such as duplicating machines, are used to provide the proper number of sets of proofs.

These galley proofs, consecutively numbered at the top so that the printer will know to which tray they belong, are first read by the compositor's proofreader. He will check as best he can against the original manuscript, query anything that he feels might be incorrect, and transfer to the proofs any unanswered editorial questions from the manuscript. These proofs are generally from six to eight inches wide, leaving sufficient space for margins in which to write the corrections.

The compositor's proofs, together with the original manuscript, are sent to the publishing house for further proofreading; this work will be described in the next chapter. They are then returned to the compositor who makes the necessary corrections and then divides the type in the galleys into pages. The designer's layout is the guide to the length of the page as well as to the insertion of special type matter such as running heads, page numbers, chapter heads, and subheads.

The proofs—called page proofs—are corrected by the compositor as well as by the publisher's proofreader. They are then returned to the compositor—sometimes accompanied by an index, which the compositor will set and which will have to be checked and corrected as was the main text of the manuscript.

The Proofreader and the Indexer

The set of proofs which has been corrected by the printer's proofreader is called the master set and is sent to the publishing house, along with at least two other sets. The master set will be read by the publisher's proofreader who checks it carefully against the manuscript to see that it conforms to the original copy. He also checks for printer's mistakes in spelling and punctuation, as well as the correctness of word division, or hyphenation, at the end of lines. In addition, the publisher's proofreader must carefully examine typographic quality—upside-down characters, damaged or broken letters, and characters of the wrong font or wrong point size that may have been mistakenly set.

Typographic quality is also checked by the designer who receives a set of galleys, but his main concern is to see that his design instructions have been followed. Typeface and size, length of lines, word spacing and let-

Proofreader's Marks

wf //	Wrong font (size or style of type)
lc	Set in LOWER CASE or LOWER CASE
caps	SET IN capitals
caps + lc	Lower Case with Initial Caps
sm. caps	SET IN small capitals
rom.	Set in roman (or regular) type
ital	Set in italic (or oblique) type
L.F.	Set in lightface type
bf	**Set in boldface type**
⌐	Move to right ⌐
⌐	⌐ Move to left
∪	Lower (letters or words)
⌐	Elevate (letters or words)
═	Straighten line (horizontally)
tr.	Transpose letters in a word
tr.	Transpose enclosed in ring matter
lead	Insert lead between lines
⅋ ld	Take out lead or tr. lead
C	Close up entirely; take out space
∪	Less space between words
eq #	Equalize space between words

l/s	LETTER-SPACE
#	Insert space (or more space)
□	Em quad space or indention
⅌	Delete, take out
stet	Let it stand — (all matter above dots)
⊄	Begin a paragraph
no ⊄	No paragraph.
run in	Run in
flush ⊄	No paragraph indention
⊙	Period
⁁	Comma
⦂	Semicolon
⊙	Colon
∨	Apostrophe or 'single quote'
∨ ∨	Quotation marks "quotes"
?/	Question mark or "query"
!/	Exclamation point
=/	Hyphen
(/)	Parentheses
[/]	Brackets
⊙	Reverse (upside-down type or cut)
⊥	Push down space or lead that prints
SP	Spell out (20 gr.)
ok w/c	OK "with corrections"
ok a/c	or "as corrected"

Example of Marked Proof

When all changes and corrections have been made on the various sets of galleys, they are coordinated and transferred to the master set which is returned, together with the manuscript, to the compositor. proofreaders' corrections marks are standard symbols, which clearly indicate to the compositor what changes should be made. It is essential that all proofreaders know these symbols, and it is most useful if the authors, too, are familiar with them.

ter spacing—these are the things he examines most carefully. He pays minute attention, too, to any special matter and display faces used in the book and to any complicated layout.

Finally, a set of galleys is sent to the author. He reads them for errors, keeping in mind that this is most probably his last chance to make corrections that he feels could improve the book. These can be in the form of deletions, additions, changes in sentence structure, and so on. New facts might have come to light between the time the book was written and the manuscript was set into type, and these might entail rather extensive revisions, just as a sentence that seemed just right when first written might seem awkward a few months later. Many authors practically rewrite their books in galleys, but they must be warned of two important factors. One is that extensive changes are time consuming and could delay publication of the book by upsetting a carefully planned schedule, sometimes even making it necessary for a compositor to supply a set of revised galleys. Second is the fact that changes are expensive to make and could cost the author a considerable amount of money. Changes in galleys are carefully distinguished between printer's errors (marked PE after each change) and author's alterations (marked AA after each change). Though the printer is responsible for the former, it is the publisher who pays for the latter, and generally a publisher, by contract, will pay no more than a sum equivalent to 10 percent of the original composition physical contact with its mother. . . . In addition the infant may reach one or both arms towards the mother. She normally reacts to this expression and gesture by going to collect her infant.

Primate Ethology

Well, I thought, I'll just give him a little hug, change his diaper, and put him down. Well, I thought wrong.

After he was changed and clean, he refused to let me out of his clutches. I tried to coax him into playing with his rubber ball or hammer and pegs while I prepared dinner, but he'd leave me for only a few seconds and then come scurrying back, tugging plaintively at my legs until I picked him up.

Bèchamel sauce is tricky enough to get right without the added handicap of stirring it while your neck is full of arms. Something had to be done. Since it was my Bèchamel sauce and my neck, I recognized that I had to do it. I gave Jerry a handful of grapes, which were Boris's favorite treat, and at this point I felt that bribery was justified.

Jerry opened his arms and held out a grape. Boris eyed him, snatched the grape, and tightened his grip around my neck. I respected the fact Boo was incorruptible but knew now that I'd have to make him an offer he couldn't refuse. Before he had an inkling of what was about to happen, I pried him loose and plomped him in Jerry's lap. He struggled with the outraged fury of the just, ignoring all grapes, all cajoling, ignoring every attention-swaying ruse in the book. And then our little fluff ball got angry.

The mature chimpanzee Cogo was kept in a compound, but he eventually broke away from it. . . . Once, in a few minutes he wrung the necks of 27 hens, 4 dwarf antelopes, and 2 ground hornbills. In the confined state Cogo was an assassin, but when he was free he was gentle, obliging, and affectionate.

The Ape People

Suddenly Boris's hair bristled; his eyes shot black lightning. He stood erect on Jerry's lap, threw his arms in the air, skinned back his lips and rapid-fired raging barks—"uh-uh-uh-uh—with goose-bumping resonance. Jerry was stunned. I was shaken. Such violent emotion, though we'd read about it, seemed incongruous with so

Galley proof showing author's alteration, printer's errors, editorial correction (A), and designer's remarks

bill, charging the author for anything above this amount.

When all changes and corrections have been made on the various sets of galleys, they are coordinated and transferred to the master set which is returned, together with the manuscript, to the compositor. Proofreaders' correction marks are standard symbols, which clearly indicate to the compositor what changes should be made. It is essential that all proofreaders know these symbols, and it is most useful if the authors, too, are familiar with them.

After the galleys have been corrected and divided into pages by the compositor, page proofs are sent to the publishing house, where they are carefully examined. The proofreader checks to see if the galley corrections have been followed, reading entire lines to see that new errors have not been made while old ones were being corrected. He or she also checks top and bottom lines of each page to make sure that no lines have been dropped during the division into pages. (The designer again checks to see that his or her instructions have been followed.)

Further editorial work is done at this point, since all the pages have been given numbers. This means that cross-references, table of contents, and lists of illustrations can be completed by the insertion of accurate page numbers. It also means that an index can be prepared.

The indexer's job is one requiring patience, skill, and accuracy. Before the actual work can begin, the indexer must know just what kind of index is required. There are several possibilities. A name index means that only names of people will be listed; a proper noun index would involve names of places, works of art or literature, and names of organizations as well as people. Most difficult of all is an index which includes concepts—i.e., censorship, poetry, colonialism, to give a few examples—and which often calls for subentries as well as main entries.

Each indexer has his or her own method of working, but in general an indexer first reads through the proofs quickly to get an idea of the nature of the work and the problems that may arise. Next, the proofs are very carefully read, and those words to be included in the index

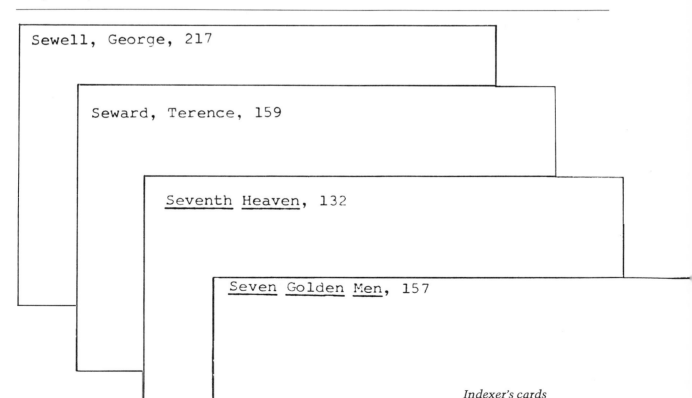

Indexer's cards

Aiken, Conrad, 9

Aldington, Richard, 85, 123, 124

Anderson, Margaret, 81, 119, 131

Anderson, Sherwood, 43-46, 48, 51, 59, 60, 63, 72, 152

    Dark Laughter, 59

    Winesburg, Ohio, 46

Ansermet, Ernest, 98, 99, 100, 114

Antheil, George, 23, 101-103, 105-110, 115, 153, 160, 162

    Ballet Méchanique, 108-110

    Symphony in F, 108

Apollinaire, Guillaume, 23

Aragon, Louis, 13

Auric, Georges, 98

Baker, Josephine, 158

Balanchine, George, 93

Barnes, Djuna, 72, 133

Handwritten designer's specifications (right margin):

Set index:

2 columns (12 × 1 × 12 picas)

10/13 Bodoni reg., c/lc × 12 picas

flush left, ragged right.

Indent sub-entries 1/m, runovers 2 ems.

first page 34 ll. per col.

full pp. 68 ll. per col.

From an index manuscript page, copy edited, with designer's specifications are underlined while concepts will be noted in the margins. After that, the indexer transfers the underlined words and noted concepts to individual 3 × 5 file cards, which also carry the corresponding page numbers. These cards are then coordinated and alphabetized; some compositors will agree to set the index from these cards, while others require that the index be typed as any other copy would be.

The index is an important part of a book and can be of enormous value to the reader. Because of this, it is essential that it be accurately prepared and painstakingly corrected once it has been composed. Some indexes are so difficult and complex that the indexer will—with good reason—be given credit in the book for his or her work.

The Printer

The printer's job is, of course, an essential one, since everything so far has led toward the transformation of the author's manuscript into a book, and this can be achieved only by printing. It is the printer's responsibility to prepare plates that will carry the images (both type and art) of the contents of the book. It is then his responsibility to print the book—that is, to transfer these images to large sheets of paper, which will be folded and bound into finished books. Machines now do much of the work that was once done by man, but the printer controls those machines and must have a thorough knowledge of their functions and how they can best be utilized.

There are several different methods by which books can be printed, each requiring a different kind of plate; the most commonly used today is called photo offset lithography, or, more simply, offset. The principle of this way of printing is the natural antipathy of grease and water. It is known as *photo* offset because the printing plates are prepared with the use of films.

The printer makes these films from the mechanicals that have been supplied by the designer. These mechanicals are mounted on a camera board and are photographed to obtain a negative film. The negative is developed and carefully examined for every detail; it is then positioned and taped onto a sheet of goldenrod, an opaque orange-yellow paper that serves as a support. This procedure is called stripping. When everything is firmly in place, the stripper cuts windows in the goldenrod paper where it covers the image areas so that light can pass through them during exposure to the plate. The result of this work is called a flat, which is the same size as the press sheet.

Proofing of these flats is generally done on blueprint paper. The blueprints are made by exposing a chemically treated paper, together with a flat, to a strong arc light in a vacuum printing frame. When developed in a liquid bath, the result is a contact print or a positive proof, from which it is possible for the designer to tell if the assembled image elements have been properly positioned, and if there are any defects in the flat. Unfortunately, the paper shrinks when it is washed during developing, so some elements—such as size and register—cannot be accurately checked.

There are two alternatives to blueprints. One of these is a vandyke, or brownprint, and the other is an Ozalid,

Stages of the Printing Process

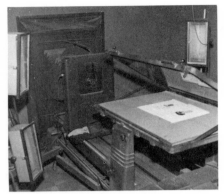

1 *Mechanical ready to be shot by camera*

2 *Negatives are developed*

3 *Negatives are stripped onto goldenrod*

4 *Flat is shot for press plates*

5 *Plates are on press*

6 *Final press sheet*

or whiteprint. This latter, because it is developed with ammonia fumes rather than a liquid, does not shrink and is thus useful in checking sizes and registers.

The actual making of offset plates is a complex process, the aim being to produce a thin sheet of metal with printing and nonprinting areas based on the principle that grease and water do not mix. Since these areas are almost level, chemical means must be employed to see that the printing areas will be water-repellent, and that the nonprinting areas will be ink-repellent.

Many different kinds of offset plates are made, but they can roughly be divided into three categories. The first, and the most commonly used, are surface plates— so called because the printing areas are on the surface. A metal sheet is coated with a light-sensitive, ink-receptive substance. There are many such substances, but the most widely used is diazo, a compound that disintegrates under exposure to light. When the plate is exposed to light through the negative film, the coating hardens and becomes insoluble in the printing areas, while remaining soft in the nonprinting areas. A water-receptive material that attaches itself only to the uncoated metal is then applied. In this way, the plate is divided into printing and nonprinting parts.

The second type of offset plate, used for longer runs and able to produce a higher quality of printing, is called deep-etch. In these plates, the greasy printing areas are very slightly below the nonprinting areas, because the light-hardened coating has been removed and chemically made ink-receptive in contrast to the wet nonprinting areas. These plates differ, too, in that they are made with film positives rather than negatives.

The third kind of offset plate is called bimetal; the advantage of these plates is their extreme durability. They are based on the principle of a light-sensitive protective coating on a metal ink-receptive base. After exposure to the film, the coating is removed from the nonprinting areas. These then receive a thin plating of copper or another water-receptive metal in an electrolytic bath. Another bath removes the remaining coating, exposing the ink-receptive metal in the printing areas.

Once the plates have been made, actual printing can begin. Printing presses are complicated machines that must perform several functions. They must be capable of holding the image carrier, the plate, firmly in position. They must be able to provide for the application of the ink essential to printing. Each press, too, must have a device for the exact placement of the paper on which the image will be printed. There must be a means of applying the pressure to print that image, and there must be a way for printed sheets to be removed as well as a place for them to be temporarily stored. In addition, each press must have room to hold blank paper and ink preparatory to use. Thus, a printing press performs many functions, either simultaneously or in a carefully planned sequence.

Presses used for offset printing are called rotary

presses: they function by means of a series of cylinders. The plates with their grease-receptive printing areas and water-receptive nonprinting areas are clamped to a plate cylinder. This cylinder rotates and comes into contact first with rollers wet by water or another dampening solution, and then with rollers wet with ink. The water prevents the oily ink from wetting the nonprinting areas.

The printing areas, now inked, rotate on their cylinder against another cylinder which carries a rubber blanket. The inked image is thus transferred, or offset, onto this blanket cylinder.

This latter cylinder, in turn, rotates against an impression cylinder. Paper, which has been lifted from a feed pile by suction, passes between the turning blanket and impression cylinders, picking up the image from the blanket before being transferred to a delivery pile.

A second method of printing is letterpress which was until recently the most widely used way of printing a book. It can be described as printing from raised surfaces which are inked and then pressed against paper on which they leave an impression. An ordinary rubber stamp is a simple example of this.

The raised surfaces include composed type and engraved illustrations. These are assembled and placed in a rectangular steel frame called a chase and locked together. In this way they can be used directly for printing, but most often they are used to make duplicate plates—more or less permanent materials from which to

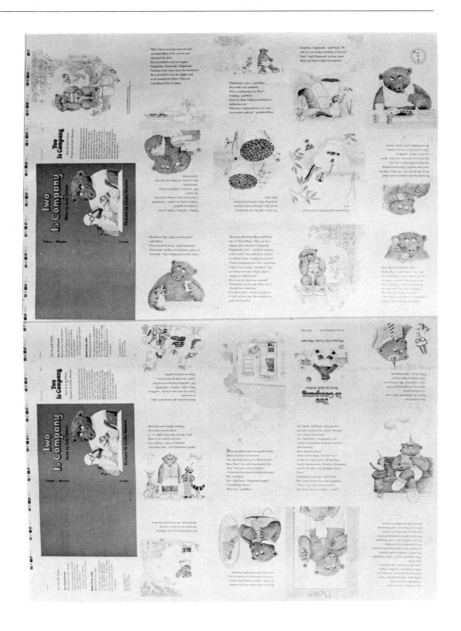

Press sheet

print a large number of copies of the book; several printings, if called for.

There are many kinds of plates or image carriers—metal, plastic, rubber, magnesium, and others—which are suitable for letterpress printing, all based on the principle of a mold which can be taken from type and illustrations and converted into permanent plates. Printing—except from metal type, which cannot be curved—is usually carried out on a rotary press.

Another method of printing, not widely used for books in the United States, is gravure. It is especially effective for the printing of photographs or other halftone copy, but it reproduces type poorly and is extremely expensive. While offset prints from almost completely flat surfaces and letterpress from raised surfaces, gravure is printed from sunken or depressed surfaces. The lines that are to print are cut below the surface of the plates.

Whatever way of printing is used—offset, letterpress, or gravure—once the printer has completed his work, the manuscript is well on its way to becoming a book. Before it can be called that, however, the large printed sheets provided by the printer must be folded, assembled in the proper sequence (gathered), and bound. Before describing this final step in the production of a book, it is best to examine the special problems involved in color printing.

The Color Printer

Printer's process color bars

Most books are printed in one color, and that color is black. However, several kinds of books call for more than one color, and the printing of these books is both more costly and more complicated than the black-and-white printing already discussed.

An extra color or extra colors can be used for merely decorative purposes, to enrich the appearance of a book, but there are many cases in which color printing is essential. Some textbooks are an example, those which include charts and graphs that become clearer in meaning with the use of color. Maps often require color printing, and an added color can be helpful in distinguishing one kind of text block from another. Children find colors attractive, and for this reason a large number of children's books are illustrated in color. Art books require color printing for the reproduction of paintings in which color plays an important part, and reproductions of color photographs enhance the value–both commercial and aesthetic–of a gift book. In a world in which we are becoming more and more accustomed to seeing images in color–black-and-white movies are already rare and black-and-white television may become so–the use of color illustrations in books, too, should be increasing, but it is actually decreasing because of the high costs of color-printing procedures.

The reasons for the high costs can be easily understood through an explanation of the two kinds of color printing: one of these is called multicolor or flat color; the other is full color or process color.

For flat-color printing, the printer will generally be provided with mechanicals for the entire book. These mechanicals consist of the art that has been preseparated by the illustrator (as described in the chapter on the illustrator), combined with the text which has been positioned and pasted in by the designer of the book.

In some cases, however, the colors have not been preseparated by the illustrator and will have to be camera-separated by the printer. In these cases, all the art and text are on one board, with no overlays. It is photographed several times in black and white, one time for each color to be used. Each negative is then opaqued–that is, the areas not wanted as part of the plate are painted out, so that each negative before platemaking will contain only those parts to be printed in any given color.

Platemaking for flat-color printing is the same as for

20%

40%

60%

80%

20%

40%

60%

80%

20%

40%

60%

80%

Screen percentages of three process colors; expanded color chart on page 152

*Preseparated artwork by
John Wallner from* Little
Fox Goes to the End of the
World *by Ann Tompert*

Black halftone separation

Red separation as prepared by artist

Red separation printed in process magenta

Yellow separation as prepared by artist

Yellow separation printed in process yellow

Blue separation as prepared by artist

Blue separation printed in cyan

Yellow and magenta together

Cyan and yellow together

Cyan, yellow and magenta

Cyan, yellow, magenta and black

Sample color swatches

black-and-white printing. However, a separate plate will be made for each color. To obtain these colors, the printer buys ink of the desired colors from an ink supplier; if special colors are required, the artist provides swatches which are matched by mixing standard inks and then given to the printer.

It is in the printing that special problems–and extra costs–arise. Each color is printed separately, which means–except in the case of multicolor presses that run several colors at the same time on different cylinders of the same machine–running the presses two, three, or four times, depending on the number of colors used. Between each press run, too, the presses must be thoroughly cleaned so that no trace is left of the last color used. This procedure is called washup.

A most serious problem, as it was for the illustrator in preseparation, is that of register. Great precision is obviously essential when any overprinting is involved, since the colors must combine exactly where indicated. Register can be faulty due to improper mounting of the plates, irregular trimming of the paper, or, above all, distortion of the paper due to moisture. This can be caused by even a slight variation of humidity in the pressroom between the printing of each color, or by application of too much water in the course of the printing.

Proper register and color can only be checked by pulling proofs on the paper that will be used for printing, and then correcting the inking, the plates themselves, or the register. This, too, is an expensive operation, requiring great care and skill.

There are methods of flat-color printing that are less costly. One is the use of the above-mentioned multicolor presses, which, because each cylinder will be using the same color, do not require washup. They also save time in that one machine, though a more complicated one, can print all the necessary colors at once. Multicolor presses are widely used now, though at one time they were economical only for rather long print runs.

Photo, out of register

Another money-saving method is called split fountain. The trough, called a fountain, from which the inks are picked up by the roller, is divided into sections, a different color in each section. The roller is inked along its length with the different colors and transfers those inks to corresponding parts of the plate. There is some danger of the inks becoming mixed, but if properly done, and if the plates can be arranged in correct sequence on the presses, split fountain color printing–because it involves fewer press runs–can constitute a considerable saving of time and money.

The second kind of color printing, full color–sometimes known as process color–is far more complex than is flat-color printing. Since it will yield a very wide range of colors, it is used for the reproduction of paintings, color photographs and other subjects which require a large number of colors for faithful reproduction.

General theories of light and color require highly technical explanations, beyond the scope of this book.

blue

green

red

Primary light colors

Simply summarized, it can be said that the three primary colors are blue, green, and red; they are called primary because a balanced mixture of these three colors produces so-called white light. The objects that we see absorb, reflect, and transmit different color components of the light in which they are seen. When we call an object green, we are saying that it reflects green light while it absorbs blue and red light.

Color filters serve to transmit selective ranges of color light. For example, a green filter transmits green light while absorbing blue and red light, just as a blue filter transmits blue light while absorbing the others. Mixtures of any two of these colors produce the colors which are basic to full-color printing: cyan, magenta, and yellow.

There are two kinds of copy used for full-color printing: the original work of art itself, or a color slide—often called a transparency—of the original. In order to make plates for full-color reproduction, the colors of the copy must first be separated by camera into each primary color.

To do this, the copy is photographed at least three times with a special lens. One lens is covered with a red filter, the second lens is covered with a green filter, and the third lens is covered with a blue filter. The red filter produces a negative of all the red light which is called a red separation negative; the green filter produces a green separation negative; and the blue filter a blue separation negative. A positive is then made of each negative. The red one produces a combination of blue and green, which is called cyan; the green produces a combination of red and blue, called magenta; the blue produces a combination of red and green, which is yellow. These are the three colors of what are called the process inks, those which combine to bring the widest possible range of colors and are thus used in full-color printing. In most cases, in addition to these three separations, a black separation will be made to add depth and brilliance to the reproduction; this is obtained by placing a red, green, and blue filter successively before the lens while the copy is photographed.

Ideally, these separations should result in a perfectly faithful reproduction of the copy, but due to imperfections in printing inks and paper, they do not, so that a great deal of correction of the negative is necessary. This is done manually, photographically, or, in recent times, electronically.

Hand correction is a very complicated task, performed by specialists who closely examine the negatives, eliminate the flaws in the film, and opaque and retouch when necessary. By dot-etching, they are able to reduce or increase the size or number of halftone dots with the use of chemicals.

Photographically, corrections can be made by masking. In this procedure, a set of separation negatives is made with special filters. These are combined with the primary set and serve to control the density, modifying or eliminating unwanted colors.

Process colors

black   cyan   magenta   yellow

Magenta

Yellow

Magenta and yellow

Cyan

Cyan and yellow

Cyan, yellow and magenta

Black

Magenta, yellow, cyan and black

Process Color Chart
Y=Yellow R=Red (magenta) B=Blue (cyan) K=Black
Various percentages of the process inks are combined to give a wide range of color; some are shown here

100Y 100R	30Y 100R	100Y 70K	100Y 100B	10Y 100B	10R 100B	100R 80K
100Y 80R	30Y 80R	100Y 50K	100Y 80B	10Y 80B	10R 80B	100R 50K
100Y 50R	30Y 50R	100Y 20K	100Y 50B	10Y 50B	10R 50B	100R 30K
100Y 30R	30Y 30R	100Y 10K	100Y 30B	10Y 30B	10R 30B	100R 10K
100Y 10R	30Y 10R	50Y 10R	100Y 10B	10Y 10B	10R 10B	10Y 100R
80Y 100R 10B	50Y 30R 10B	80Y 10R 50K	50Y 10R 50B	80B 20K	10R 10B 50K	30R 50K
80Y 50R 10B	30Y 30R 10K	50Y 10R 80B	50Y 10R 30B	80B 80K	50R 50B 50K	30R 10K
100Y 100R 50B	30Y 80R 10K	100Y 100B 70K	50Y 10R 100B	50R 100B 70K	50R 100B 10K	100R 100B

Today, manual and photographic correction can be eliminated by the use of electronic color scanners, which both separate and balance the colors.

Plates for full-color printing are made photomechanically. The corrected negatives are exposed against sensitized film to make positives. The positives are then placed against another film with a halftone screen in between them. The resultant screened halftone negatives are used to make the plates. Since the colored dots generally print alongside each other, the halftone screens are usually placed at different angles for each color.

For full-color printing, there will be as many press runs as there are colors. As in flat-color printing, register is of very great importance as is the proper application of ink to the plates.

The proofs from which the printer can check and control his work are called progressives. Each of the colors used is shown singly and in combination. There will be a yellow proof and a magenta proof; then a proof of yellow and magenta together. Then there will be a cyan proof, followed by a yellow, magenta, and cyan proof. Then a black proof will be made, followed by a proof of all four colors together.

Preparation and correction of these progressives is a costly and painstaking job, as well as a crucial one. Not only will the printer himself check them for color balance and fidelity to the original, but usually the production manager of the publishing house as well as the ar-

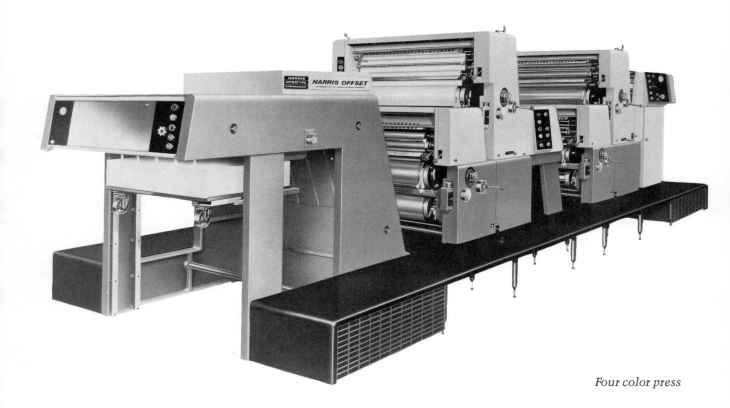

Four color press

tist, when possible, will come to the pressroom to control the printing and see that the plates or inks, when faulty, are modified to ensure as faithful a reproduction as possible. Each color plate is minutely examined, as is the color combination as well as the register. With today's technology and skills, good full-color printing can come close to the original work, but only if it is carefully planned, prepared, and controlled.

The Binder

Binding is the final step in the production of a book. Its purpose is to bring and hold together the printed pages of the book in the proper sequence, in some sort of permanent form, so that they will be protected within a case and can be read comfortably. The binder's job involves a mechanically complex operation, but it is relatively simple to understand, since each step leads logically to the final purpose. There are many such steps, and it is best to describe them one by one, though there are many machines used along the way that can carry out two or even more of them in one operation.

There are two basic methods of bookbinding: edition binding and perfect binding. They differ largely in that the pages are held together by sewing in the former and by an adhesive in the latter.

The first step for both methods is the folding of the printed sheets, according to the predetermined imposition. Once the sheets have been folded, they are called signatures. They generally contain sixteen or thirty-two pages. These individual signatures are then gathered: that is, they will be assembled in the proper sequence for the book.

It is in the next step that the major differences between edition binding and perfect binding occur. Edition-bound books are sewed, most often by a method called Smyth sewing. A thread of cotton—or occasionally nylon—is passed through the fold of each signature. It is then secured and passed through the stitches of other signatures so that all are joined together. This way of joining the signatures enables the book to be opened flat. Another method, known as side sewing, does not allow this. In this method, used generally for short books, often of no more than one signature, the thread is passed through the entire book from the side. An advantage of side sewing is that it is less expensive than Smyth sewing; it is also very strong, but its very strength prevents the book from being opened flat.

In perfect binding, there is no sewing at all. Once used only for paperbacks and inexpensive books, it has in recent years been greatly improved, though it is still doubtful that perfect binding can ever be as durable as edition binding.

The backs of the signatures—the folding edges—are trimmed off, and the entire book becomes individual leaves. These edges are then made coarse, in order to increase the surface for the gluing which follows. Not

Perfect Binding

Back of signatures being trimmed off   *Gluing*   *Cover being attached*

only are one or two films of a flexible adhesive applied to the edges, but a coarsely woven fabric is often attached to serve as added reinforcement.

The next step in the binding process, called smashing, is necessary only for edition binding. Since the back of the book has become slightly thicker because of the sewing thread, it must be brought to uniform thickness. This is accomplished by means of vertical presses that apply enormous pressure to the gathered signatures, squeezing out the air and compressing the pages firmly.

Gluing, which has already been done for perfect binding, follows smashing. In this process, a thin coat of flexible glue is applied to hold the signatures in place.

Next, the signatures are trimmed: that is, they are cut to their final size by means of trimming machines. The top, front, and bottom folds—all but the back ones—are opened up so that it will be possible to turn the pages.

At this point, it is possible to color the top edge of the book if desired. This procedure is called staining. Putting a top stain on a book can be attractive aesthetically; it also makes the book look cleaner, and serves to make the edges of the paper dust-resistant. Staining is done by brushing, sponging, or spraying the edges of the signatures with a water-soluble dye of any color.

The next two steps are commonly done on the same machine and concern preparation of the spine of the book; their aim is to enable the fastened-together signatures to be secured tightly within the covers.

The first of these two steps is called rounding. The backbone of the signatures is passed through a pair of rollers, which slightly rounds it, ensuring that the front edge of the book will remain under the covers and not protrude. This procedure, too, allows the covers to open and close easily.

The second of these steps is called backing, another way of making sure that the book will not slip out of its covers. By slightly widening and spreading out the back edge, backing provides joints for the book. In a way, it creates a sort of shoulder against which the covers of the book can fit.

The final step before actually putting the book in its covers now takes place. It is called lining up and is often combined with the two previous operations. In lining up, one or more strips of gauze, known as crash or

1 *Press sheets are folded into signatures*

2 *Signatures are gathered*

3 *Signatures are Smyth sewn*

4 *Sewn signatures are reinforced with glue*

5 *Sewn signatures are trimmed*

Sewn signatures are rounded (left) and backed with paper (right); headbands are attached here

6

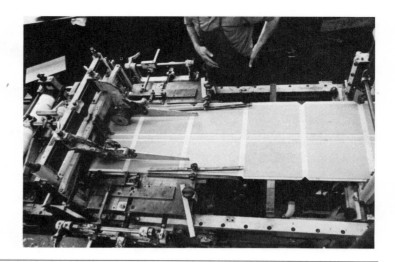

7 *Cases are made and stamped*

8 *Signatures are cased-in*

9 *Books are jacketed, ready for shipping*

super, are glued to the back edge of the book. This cloth extends outward from both sides of the backbone. Very often, too, a strip of strong paper is also applied along the backbone. In this way the back of the book is reinforced and provided with a firm connection which will enable it to be attached to the covers.

Many years ago, headbands were attached to the backbone, extending slightly above the book, to protect the edges of fine binding materials such as leather. Today, headbands, though used, serve only a decorative purpose and are nothing more than very small pieces of cloth, woven with colored thread, which are pasted to the lining material and protrude slightly to give a look of elegance to the book.

Whether sewn or glued together, the pages are now ready to be put between covers; the covers themselves are prepared while the sheets are folded, gathered, lined up, and so on, so that both are ready at the same time.

These covers—also called cases—serve several functions. They protect the book, allow it to stand on a shelf in a rigid positon, make it durable, enhance its beauty, and provide other areas for information and identification.

Each cover consists of four parts: there are two boards, paper to line the backbone or spine, which is called backlining, and the cover material itself.

The boards are cut to a size slightly greater than that of the trim size of the book so that there will be a small, protective overlap. They are of a heavy cardboard, the

Casemaking

1 *Boards are glued in position on cloth*

2 *Cloth is cut and turned in*

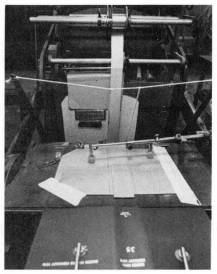

3 *Cases are stamped*

4 *Three piece case (left) and one piece case (right), ready for casing-in*

strongest kind of which is called binder's board.

A heavy paper serves for the backlining. It is cut to a height slightly greater than that of the trim size and slightly wider than the bulk of the pages.

The cover material may be of cloth, plastic, or paper, or a combination of cloth and paper. Cloth is both the most durable and the most expensive covering, and it is available in many grades, colors, and finishes. Often a publisher will choose to use cloth for the center of the cover—that part which covers the spine and overlaps around the sides, which are subject to most wear—and paper for the rest of the cover in order to save money. The choice of the cover material is made by the designer of the book, with both aesthetic and economic considerations taken into account.

This cover material is cut to somewhat larger size than the boards to allow for folding over the edges (turn-in) and for extra material necessary for the joints.

Once they have been chosen and cut, the parts of the cover are assembled. The inside of the cover material is coated with an adhesive; the boards and backlining are placed in proper position; and the extra material is folded over the edges by small rollers. All is then pressed firmly together.

Except for the addition of decorative or informative elements, the cover is finished. The information required is supplied by the editorial department, while its manner of presentation and any decorative aspects are decided upon by the designer.

Information, to be placed on the spine, generally includes the name of the author, the title of the book, and the name of the publisher. The back of the cover is generally blank, while the front cover might include a decoration or a symbol—even the author's initials—for the book. Since jackets are used to convey the feeling of the book, covers tend to be simple. There are, however, some exceptions, such as the occasional use of letterpress or offset to print elaborate illustrations on the cover material. In addition, covers of some books, which use no jackets, are preprinted.

For the most part, printed matter and decorations are applied to the covers by means of stamping; there are two kinds of stamping, hot stamping and cold stamping. Both make use of an etched plate called a binding die. Hot stamping is achieved by pressing the die against foil, or a leaf which comes in a large number of different colors. The metal die is heated, and the image is transferred to the cover material by means of heat. Hot stamping also includes blind stamping, which is the same process but without the use of foil. The impression is achieved by a difference in elevation, or relief images.

Cold stamping employs ink rather than foil. A deeply etched plate—the binding die—is inked, and the image is transferred by great pressure sufficient to penetrate the cloth or paper cover material. This process is the same as ordinary letterpress, except that the pressure applied is far greater.

Binding die

The book and its cover are now ready to be joined; this procedure is called casing-in. The flat back of the case is slightly rounded by a heated bar, which corresponds in shape to the rounded backbone of the book. The outer leaves of the endpapers are covered with a glue or paste. The case is then placed around the book so that the boards are on the two endpapers, and two thin uncovered strips of the covering material are positioned over the joints of the book. The cased-in book is now firmly pressed to prevent warping of the boards. The press is hydraulic, and pressure is applied until the adhesive on the endpapers dries completely.

The result is a finished book. As they come off the production line, the books are examined for faults and then jacketed, either by machine or by hand. It has been a long time between the author's conception of the work and the finished product.

Now the book must be publicized and promoted; it must be shipped and sold. Above all, it must be read.

From the Warehouse to the Bookstore

Once the book has been printed, bound, and jacketed, there remains the final—and all-important—job of doing everything to see that it is sold to and read by as many people as possible. The first step is to move the books from the warehouse to the stores; the second will be to move them from the stores into the homes of the customers. These two goals are worked on simultaneously in many ways, but they can be most clearly discussed separately.

It is primarily the task of the salesman to see that the book reaches the stores. The salesman first learns about the book at a meeting called a sales conference—usually held before the book is finished. Most publishers divide their list into two seasons: there is the fall list which roughly includes books published between July and the end of December; and the spring list which includes those published between January and the end of June.

The sales conference for the fall list generally takes place in May, while the conference for the spring list takes place in December.

Present at these meetings are many members of the publishing house: members of the editorial staff, the publicity department, representatives of the advertising agency, and, of course, the entire sales force. In the course of these conferences which, depending on the size of the list, can last one, two, or even three days, future books are discussed and presented to the salesmen so that they may have all the information necessary to sell the books.

Each title—and it is essential to remember that each title is a distinct product, different from all others—is presented to these salesmen by an editor, the publisher, or, in some cases, the sales manager, the man or woman who directs and coordinates the activities of the entire sales force. These presentations are generally made in the order in which each book appears in the catalog of future titles which has been prepared in the publishing house before the sales conference and which will be an important sales tool.

The salesman will want to know just what the book is about and, essentially, why a bookstore, and in the end a customer, should buy it. In other words, the salesmen want a "handle" for each book. This means quite simply a short (the shorter the better) description of those qualities that should make a book salable. For example, it is the first biography of some prominent and

Publishers' catalogs

interesting figure; it is a book that has been sold to the movies; it is a work of literature of such importance that it is certain to be widely reviewed and praised....

Information about the author is useful, and a book's special appeal to a specific area of the country—whether it be the author's home where he is well known, or the setting of the book—will be discussed. The salesmen will want to know what the publicity department plans to do for the book, whether or not excerpts from it have been sold to a magazine for publication before the book is published, whether or not it is a book club selection, and what the advertising budget will be. Essential to the salesmen, too, is knowledge of the size of the first printing. This could be discussed and even revised at sales conference, depending upon the reactions of those attending the meeting to any given title, but usually the number of copies to be printed has been determined in advance. This figure is an important one to the salesmen since it reflects the publisher's confidence in the book's salability.

Of great importance is the presentation of each jacket to the members of the sales conference. Usually, it is a color proof of the jacket that is prepared and shown so that suggestions made by the sales staff and others can be followed before the jacket is printed. Occasionally, the salesmen will be presented with a number of different sketches for a title, and the selection of what will be the final jacket will be discussed by all the members of the conference. A most effective jacket might be the result of such an exchange of ideas.

The sales conference is basically a period set aside for an exchange of ideas, of ways in which a title can best be sold to the stores. By the end of these meetings, the salesmen should be fully prepared to present each book, prepared to tell each bookstore owner or buyer why he or she should buy copies of each title, prepared, too, to answer any question that might be asked. Above all, the presentation of a book at sales conference should generate interest. The jacket might be good, the "handle" useful, but the enthusiasm that the man or woman—usually the editor—can convey to the salesmen can well mean the difference, in the end, between a book that sells well or one that sells poorly.

Once the sales meetings are over, the salesman

gathers together his materials in preparation for his selling trip. These materials consist of a jacket (or proof of one) for each book, a catalog of all the new titles as well as the backlist (those books published in the past that might be reordered), and a number of order forms. In the case of heavily illustrated books, it could be useful to carry along a sample illustration or two; in the case of children's books, an unbound copy of the book itself is helpful since the appearance of the entire book is of great importance to a bookseller.

Most salesmen are "house" men; that is, they sell for only one publisher who pays a salary, expenses, and often a commission on sales. There are, however, commission salesmen who sell for a number of different publishers—the smaller publishers who cannot afford to keep a full-time sales force. These commission salesmen pay their own expenses and receive as compensation a percentage of the sales. This commission is generally between 10 and 12½ percent of the wholesale price on sales to bookstores and between 5 and 7½ percent of the wholesale price to jobbers.

All of these salesmen sell to three basic types of accounts. First of all, there are the bookstores—small personal ones, as well as large chains which usually buy their books through one central office. Then, there are the jobbers who buy in large quantities and in turn sell these books to retail stores and libraries. Many small shops prefer to buy from jobbers since these latter carry books of all publishers, and thus billing and accounting

FOR OFFICE USE ONLY

H C 7

TERMS: 2/10 EOM, NET 30 F.O.B. SHIPPING POINT.

MINIMUM TRADE ORDER $5.00 NET Prices subject to change without notice.

☐ PAYMENT ENCLOSED $ _____
☐ CHARGE MY ESTABLISHED ACCOUNT
☐ NEW ACCOUNTS PLEASE SUBMIT TRADE AND BANKING REFERENCE
PRE PAYMENT OF YOUR FIRST ORDER WILL INSURE PROMPT DELIVERY

BACK ORDER INSTRUCTIONS
☐ USUAL—BILL AND SHIP AS READY
☐ CANCEL ALL UNAVAILABLE BOOKS
☐ CANCEL PREVIOUS BACK ORDER FOR TITLES ON THIS ORDER
☐ CANCEL ALL UNAVAILABLE BOOKS EXCEPT NEW PUBS AS OF:

ISBN PREFIX: 0—517

BUYER

BUYERS PHONE

SALES REP. AND NUMBER

BILL TO:
ADDRESS
CITY & STATE
MARK FOR: ZIP
SHIP TO
MARK FOR: ZIP

ORDER NO. | DEPT. NO. | DISCOUNT | WHEN SHIP | SHIP VIA | SPECIAL INSTRUCTIONS

INVOICE NO.

Previously Announced

518740	An Ancient World Preserved, *Engel*	9.95
525437	Disaster Illust., *Gelman & Jackson* (H) p	4.95
525429	Disaster Illust., *Gelman & Jackson* (H)	10.95
526123	Front Page 1975 . . . . . . p	9.95
525852	Great Movie Cartoon Parade, *Rider* p	9.95
52550X	In the Ring of the Rise, *Marinaro* .	12.95
52533X	Miracle Houseplants, *Elbert* . . p	6.95
525321	Miracle Houseplants, *Elbert* . .	12.95
525828	Photograph. Amer., *Hornby et al* .	15.95
524937	Prints of Reg. Marsh, *Sasowsky* (CNP)	15.00
516977	R. A. Parker's Illust. Frankenstein, *Parker* . . . . . (CNP) p	5.95

August

527863	American Artist: Norman Rockwell p	1.25
527359	Artist and Computer, *Leavitt* . (H) p	4.95
525909	Creat. Art with Br. Dough, *Meilach* p	4.95
525895	Creat. Art with Br. Dough, *Meilach* .	7.95
52631X	Creative Handicrafts Course, *Olsheim* p	5.95
526271	House Book, *Conran*	30.00
526360	How to Meditate Without Attending a TM Class, *Akins & Nurnberg* . .	6.95
526433	Illustr. Cat: Poster Bk., *Suares, Chwast & Maloney* . . . . (H) p	5.95
526441	Illustr. Cat: Poster Bk., *Suares, Chwast & Maloney* . . . . (H)	10.95
527324	Joy of Sex and More Joy, *Comfort* (2 vols., boxed gift ed.) . . .	19.95
528002	Knit and Crochet, Vol. 2, *Mon Tricot*	1.98
527448	Lettering Design, *Harvey* . . (B)	10.95
526352	Making Cheeses at Home, *Ogilvy* .	5.95
526662	Mod. Col. Dolls, *Fainges* . .	17.95
526131	MGM Story, *Eames* (paper ed.) . p	9.95
526522	Offic. Tartan Map Chart, *Dunbar & Pottinger* . . . . . . p	2.95
528207	Popeye the Sailor 1936-37, *Segar* . p	7.95
526182	Prepar. Art. for Repro., *Cherry* .	5.95
526417	Rolling Stones, *Carr* . . . . . p	6.95
526425	Rolling Stones, *Carr* . . . . (H)	12.95
526840	Savoy Cocktail Book, *Craddock* .	6.95
526190	Scandinavian Cooking, *Lundberg* .	3.95
527340	Terry and the Pirates: Enter the Dragon Lady, *Caniff* . . . . . . p	6.95
527332	Terry and the Pirates: Meet Burma, *Caniff* . . . . p	6.95
525917	This is Australia, *Brasch* . . .	24.95
517213	Writing Master's Amusement, *Holbrook* (Imprint Society)	45.00

September

527413	Annot. Christmas Carol, *Hearn* (CNP) until 12/31	12.95
	thereafter	15.00
526794	Aphrodisiac, *Boyce* . . . . p	4.95
526786	Aphrodisiac, *Boyce*	7.95
528088	Art of F. Booth, *Calkins & Nicholson* .	7.95
526808	Auth. Wild West, *Horan* . . .	12.95
528185	Auth. Wild West, *Horan* (Ltd. Ed.)	100.00
528029	Best of Buster, *Anobile* . . . p	5.95
528010	Best of Buster, *Anobile*	12.95

526220	Collect. & Restor. Wicker Furn., *Saunders*	6.95
527375	Consumer's Dict. of Cosmetic Ingred., Rev. Ed., *Winter* . . . . p	4.95
527367	Consumer's Dict. of Cosmetic Ingred., Rev. Ed., *Winter*	7.95
528134	Edw. Whitefield, *Norton* (Imp. Soc.)	45.00
526255	A Good Age, *Comfort*	9.95
526484	Gustav Klimt: Poster Book . (H) p	5.95
526298	Heraldic Imagination, *Dennys* . (CNP)	15.00
526492	Intro. Ballet, *Clark & Crisp* . (H) p	3.95
526506	Intro. Ballet, *Clark & Crisp* . . (H)	7.95
52497X	L. Carroll Observ., *Guiliano* (CNP)	12.95
526328	Mating Game, *Burton*	12.95
526115	Nicolas de Stael (QLP) *Dumer* .	4.95
526697	No He's not a Monkey, *Mundis* .	6.95
52791X	125 Famous Pages fr. the NY Times: 1850-1976 . . . . . . p	3.95

October

528096	Amer. Company, *McCann & Scammet*	8.95
527219	Antiq. Shops & Dealers USA, *Doherty* p	6.95
52614X	Compl. Bk of Houseplants & Indoor Garden., *Steffek*	16.95
52726X	Fabric of the Universe, *Postel* . p	5.95
527356	Fabric of the Universe, *Postel* . .	9.95
526824	Help. Yr. Alcoholic, *Fajardo* . .	7.95
52788X	Here's to the Friars, *Adams* . .	8.95
526379	Hollywood Costume Design, *Chierichetti* (H) until 12/31	12.95
	thereafter	15.00
524988	Icart, *Schnessel* . (CNP) until 12/31	17.95
	thereafter	19.95
527421	Illustr. Edgar Allan Poe, *Sätty* . (CNP)	12.95
527383	Kovels' Compl. Antiq. Price List, 9th Ed., *Kovels* . . . . . . p	6.95
521091	Lore of Sport Fishing, *Moss* . .	29.95
526611	Made in Occupied Japan, *Klamkin* p	6.95
526603	Made in Occupied Japan, *Klamkin* .	9.95
527995	Masada Plan, *Harris*	8.95
525526	Naked and the Nude: Hollywood Years, (deluxe trade ed.) . . . . p	2.95
528142	Royal Crown Derby, *Twitchett & Bailey* (CNP)	15.00
52662X	Rule by Proxy, *Ducker*	8.95
525615	Ships' Figureheads, *Norton* . (B)	10.00
527286	Stained Glass, *Lee et al* until 12/31	35.00
	thereafter	39.95
52810X	Very Rich, *Thorndike* . until 12/31	24.95
	thereafter	29.95
528045	World's Greatest Magic, *Clark* .	14.95

November

524708	American Heirloom Bargello, *Hines* p	5.95
524694	American Heirloom Bargello, *Hines* .	7.95
526549	Antique Jewelry, *Goldemberg* . p	5.95
526530	Antique Jewelry, *Goldemberg* . .	8.95
526107	Art of Tin Toy, *Pressland* until 12/31	32.50
	thereafter	35.00
527278	At This Point in Rhyme, *Harburg* .	5.95
523922	Decorating Glass, *Rothenberg* . . p	4.95
523914	Decorating Glass, *Rothenberg* . .	6.95
521792	Fire Engines, Fire Fighters, *Ditzel* .	19.95
518724	Last Primitive Peoples, *Brain* . .	14.95
527243	Offic. Encyc. of Bridge, 3rd Rev. Ed., *Truscott, et al.*	14.95
520206	Pict. Hist. of the Russian Theatre, *Marshall*	14.95
518759	Thirty Centuries Under the Sea, *Dumas*	9.95

Children's Books

528193	Baber's Mother Goose Nurs. Rhym. (Sept.) (By)	4.95
526050	The Bear and the Fly, *Winter* (July) .	4.95
526204	Books: From Writer to Reader, *Greenfeld* (Oct.)	8.95
52600X	Little Fox Goes to the End of the World, *Tompert* (Aug.)	6.95
526158	Mr. Tamarin's Trees, *Ernst* (July) .	5.95
526042	The Rats Who Lived in the Delicatessen, *Berson* (Aug.)	5.95
526212	Toliver's Secret, *Brady* (Sept.) . .	6.95
526018	Two is Company, *Delton* (Aug.) .	4.95

SPORTS CAR PRESS

526832	How to Enjoy Sports on TV, *Tuite* (Oct.) . . . . p	3.95

Modern Sports Car Series

526727	Collect. Post WW II Cars for Fun— Profit?, *Gotthainer* (Jan.) . . p	3.95

Modern Aircraft Series

526409	Aircraft Metalwork, *Dwiggins* (Sept.) p	3.95
509016	Aircraft Woodwork, 2nd Ed., *Spencer* (Aug.) . . . . . . p	3.95
509288	Single-Engine Cessnas, 2nd Ed., (completely revised), *Christy* (Aug.) . p	3.95

Item No.	Quan.	Title	Price

Publisher's order form

procedures are simplified. The jobbers, too, are generally located in or close to large cities where they have their warehouses, so they can usually supply books more quickly than can individual publishers. The third type of account is the library. Libraries most often buy from jobbers, but certain library systems prefer to purchase their books directly from the publisher. Libraries constitute 85 percent of the market for children's books and approximately 10 percent of adult books.

By the time he is ready to begin his selling trip, the salesman should be thoroughly familiar with each title he will present to the booksellers. The shorter, more concise, and more informative his presentation is, the better he is able to sell the right number of copies to each store. Because of the large number of books carried by each salesman, there is a strictly limited amount of time that can be devoted to any single title. Within this limited amount of time, the bookstore buyer will want to know, just as the salesman wanted to know from the publisher, just how he can best sell each title to his customers. Through an annual convention held by the American Booksellers Association, attended by a large number of booksellers, publishers, and publishers' representatives, booksellers are able to learn not only what books are coming from all publishers, but which of that number will be highlighted, and how each publisher will aid and support–through promotion, publicity, and advertising–those titles. However, the personal touch of the individual salesmen plays an important part in the decisions of each bookstore buyer. The salesman must know the individual needs of each bookstore—each shop has its own character; the store's buyer must have confidence in the reliability and integrity of each salesman.

The larger the order that a shop or jobber gives, the greater the discount he receives. A usual discount would be 25 percent for an order of a single copy of a book, and over 40 percent for a very substantial order. The jobber discount is, of course, higher, averaging 46 percent, since the jobber himself will be selling books to retailers at a discount.

Nonetheless, it is not to the publisher's advantage to sell an unrealistically high number of copies of a book, and because of this a wise salesman will make no effort to oversell any one title. The reason for this is that all books sold to a bookstore are returnable: that is, the copies not sold by a store can be returned to the publisher for full credit. The salesmen may place a very large number of copies of any one title in the stores only to find that they remain unsold to customers and are eventually returned to the publisher. Obviously, unless the salesman keeps in touch with the stores to find out if the books are moving out of the stores and into the hands of customers, and conveys this information to the publisher, the latter could bring out a second printing of a title when the first was far from sold out.

Overbuying, in spite of return privileges, is unprofitable for the bookseller as well, since there are certain conditions attached to the return of books to the publisher. A soiled or damaged book cannot be returned for credit; there is a time limit for returns; and return shipping costs must be paid for by the bookseller. In addition, the amount of paper work involved can be more time-consuming than it is worth. As careful as salesmen and booksellers are, approximately 20 percent of all books sold to bookstores in the United States are eventually returned to the publishers.

The book salesman is an essential, vital link between the publishing house and the bookseller. He is important not only as the person who sells books, but also as the man or woman in the best position to carry information from publisher to bookseller *and* from bookseller to publisher, thus enabling both to perform their jobs better.

From the Bookstore to the Reader

Once the book has been sold to the stores—and usually well before this—the publicity department begins working (together with other members of the publishing house, when necessary) to do everything possible to see that the books move out of the stores and into the readers' homes. When the question is asked, "What makes a book sell?" the usual reply is "word of mouth," and generating word of mouth is the job of the publicity department. The original product, the book itself, should be so interesting and informative that it will lead one reader to recommend it to another, but the initial interest in the book must be stimulated by the publicity department of the publishing house.

Ideally, the publicity director should be intelligent, with an attractive personality (for his or her work is public relations) and a deep interest in books. He or she should have contacts with newspaper, magazine, and television people, and should preferably be on good terms with book reviewers. Above all, however, a publicity director must be creative and imaginative, because a new approach or a new idea to be used in publicizing the book could well mean the difference between its commercial success and failure. It is very often impossible to explain why one book sells and another doesn't, but the publicity director must draw on all his or her skills and imagination to call attention to the publication–and merits–of each book.

All these efforts fall within the scope of spreading word of mouth, and the almost infinite ways of achieving this are impossible to discuss here, since each book is a unique product and requires–ideally–a unique approach. Nonetheless, there are a few basic steps essential to the publication of any book, and these, with a brief look at others, are worth describing.

The most important tool in publicizing a book is the book itself, because only the book itself can stimulate the necessary enthusiasm. It is important that the publicity director, or at least a member of the staff, read the book either in manuscript or in galleys. This is obviously not always possible–a large house publishes very many books–but it is desirable, and a book should at least be skimmed even if not carefully read. In this way, the publicity department is certainly better able to generate interest in the book–that is, out of its own enthusiasm.

There are basically two areas of book publicity:

TRADE NEWS
Editor:
Robert Dahlin

Ladies and Gentlemen: In the Center Ring . . .
Hawthorn Makes Ready to Send in the Clowns

The world's romance with clowns is an affair spiced with pratfalls and guffaws, but it must be one from the heart: It's been going on for centuries. The latest evidence of it is a picture history-cum-personality book coming from Hawthorn in October, called simply "Clowns." John Towsen, a young man with a yen to clown himself, is the author.

"My whole life has been pointing in the direction of clowning, I guess," Towsen told *PW*. "I started acting at the age of seven on Red Skelton's television show." For about seven years, young Towsen appeared in some 40 TV shows, with commercials on the side, until his parents decreed that he should retire at 14 and live a normal life. "I

couple of years now. I've been doing a lot more writing than performing." And Towsen has found that a typewriter is not necessarily a satisfactory instrument for a clown. "I'm not sure I ever want to see one again," he contends.

" 'Clowns' is large in scope," Towsen says. "I don't think anything like it has been written before." Some of the earlier authors on the subject haven't been sufficiently immersed in the tradition of theater and clowning, he feels. "I did a lot of research, more than I'd planned." Nevertheless, Towsen doesn't claim the book is definitive. "It couldn't be, in this number of pages." ("Clowns" will have 356 pages, 200 black-and-white photographs, period

hands, said the opposite of what they meant. There are Hopi Indian clowns who poke fun at holy dancers. Clowns are satirical and recognized as such. They are a safety valve that keeps a balance between the sacred and the profane."

Towsen also points to the court jesters, another species of clowns. They performed at a time when parliaments and democratic processes didn't exist, he says. "They served as political satirists and a moderating influence on the king."

The book is well-timed for a new interest in clowns, Towsen feels. "There have been declines and revivals of clowning all through history," he says. "The last decline was about 30 years

From the "Trade News" column in Publishers Weekly

through reviews and book news columns in newspapers and magazines, and "off the book page," as it is popularly called—that is, anything other than book reviews or book news. Procedures for this first method of publicizing a book are pretty much standard. A book might first be announced by means of a press release: a short statement is sent to magazines and newspapers, most importantly *Publishers Weekly*, the industry's weekly magazine, saying that a certain book by a certain author dealing with a certain subject will be published by a certain publisher at a certain date. Most likely, this will be the first public announcement of the book and publication of this release in *Publishers Weekly* could well stimulate interest. (It also might, coincidentally, cancel or speed up another publisher's plans to bring out a work on the same subject.)

Formally, work can begin with the arrival of galleys. As a matter of routine, specially bound sets of these proofs are sent to those magazines whose opinions booksellers and librarians will consider when buying books. These periodicals, whose reviews will be printed well before the book is published, can be most influential in launching a book. A good review in these not only serves to move books into the stores, but it can also engender enthusiasm in the publishing house itself.

In addition, these bound galleys are sent to major newspapers and magazines which need a long time to prepare their reviews. Finally, a limited number of bound galleys are sent to influential people who might have a special interest in the book, among them noted figures who could supply laudatory quotations which can be used for advertising or for the jacket of the book.

With the sending of bound galleys, the process of word of mouth begins. The next step begins with the arrival of finished books. Each house has a list of reviewers and literary editors of newspapers and magazines to whom books are sent for review. Usually, a catalog is sent to these people several weeks or months before publication. The catalog describes the books, and along with it the publicity department will enclose a checklist of all the titles to be published. The reviewer examines the catalog and marks on the checklist those books he or she would be interested in reviewing. The checklist is returned to the publicity

PW FORECASTS

EDITOR: BARBARA A. BANNON

Nonfiction: Albert H. Johnston

Fiction: Barbara A. Bannon

Children's Books: Jean Mercier

Paperbacks: Genevieve Stuttaford

NONFICTION

HORSE FEVER.
William Murray. Dodd, Mead. $7.95
ISBN 0-396-07336-0
Murray's a *New Yorker* writer, novelist and something else: he follows the horses. Here in 21 lively "takes" is his behind-the-scenes description of his experiences at a "meet"
track

and their elders. He tells stories about grandparents who were members of his flock (two grandmothers, one a "drag"—another, 92, "lovely"). He visits a Wisconsin farm and a child asks, "Grandma, why isn't milk green?"—a question that illustrates what perhaps grandparents wondering.

lust had been set. His story of his boyhood—truancy, runaway spells, traumatic experiences as stepson of a migratory worker in Nevada and the West—is affecting and explains about him. Excerpt

From the "PW Forecasts" section, Publishers Weekly

Publishers Weekly

JULY 5, 1976 / ISSN 0000-0019 VOL. 210 NO. 1
ABA CONVENTION IN CHICAGO
BOOK DESIGN AND MANUFACTURING

department, which keeps records of which books to send to which reviewers.

The general review list is usually not enough, however. Each book being an individual case, the publicity department makes use of lists of influential people who might, because of the nature of the book, be especially interested in the subject, experts in certain fields, friends and colleagues of the author who might be useful in promoting the book, and so on. The total number of free books distributed by the publicity department might be as few as fifty or as many as several hundred.

Along with the book itself, it is common to enclose a news release and a photo. The release will briefly describe the book and its author, and the photo–hopefully

Bound book and publisher's news release

NEWS

INSANITY INSIDE OUT

by Kenneth Donaldson

"A BRAVE BOOK,
A SHOCKING STORY....
A VINDICATION FOR US ALL."

Senator Frank E. Moss, Chairman
Subcommittee on Long-Term Care
Senate Special Committee on Aging

photo © *The Washington Post*

It was just around sunset, December 10,.1956, and Kenneth
Donaldson, down from Philadelphia for a short visit with his parents in
Florida before starting a new job, was about to sit down to dinner with the
family. A knock at the screen door and two men in sport shirts appeared.
"You are under arrest," they told Donaldson.

"For what?" he said.

"Somebody told the sheriff some things and he got an order from
the judge," was the answer. "We want to talk to you at the jail."

With no more explanation than that, Kenneth Donaldson found
himself, that night, in the "hole" of the Pinellas County jail, believing
that he must be the butt of some practical joke the locals had invented to
initiate a visiting Yankee. But no humor was intended, and, unbelieveably,
Donaldson, having committed no crime and fully able to function as a responsible member of society, was not to experience another moment of freedom
for fifteen years. Ultimately, the Supreme Court of the United States, handed
down a ruling on the "Donaldson case" which may prove the most important for
mental patients in the history of the Republic. It was a landmark case that

to be used in a newspaper or magazine—will be of the author, the jacket of the book, or possibly of an illustration from the book.

Because of the huge number of books published each year and the strictly limited amount of review space available, merely sending out galleys or books and releases and photographs is not enough. Reviewers and editors are flooded with books and have the difficult task of choosing which ones to review. They will have to pay attention to works by well-known authors, and they will want to review those titles of special interest to themselves, keeping in mind that their book review sections must be balanced with a mixture of fiction, poetry, biography, current affairs, history, and so on.

However, the reviewer or book editor can use help in selecting books for review, and this help can be provided by the publicity department. If it is at all possible, the publicity director should personally see the book editor, frankly and honestly discussing the list, and pointing out the highlights. A competent publicity director knows that not every reviewer can review every book and knows, too, which books will most likely interest which reviewer. His or her guidance can be invaluable. Sometimes the editor or the publisher will either write to or see a reviewer: this special effort, if not used too often, can be helpful in obtaining a review by demonstrating an extra degree of enthusiasm. The importance of this enthusiasm, whether it comes from the publicity department, the editor, or the publisher, cannot be stressed too highly. And it is surprising how many books are helped by word of mouth spread by members of a publishing house other than the one which has published the book.

Everything discussed above is, more or less, routine work for a publicity department. It essentially consists of taking steps to see that books are reviewed or mentioned on the book pages of magazines and newspapers.

Though there is no doubt that good reviews are of great importance, it is also true that poor reviews don't necessarily mean that a book will not sell. If the author has a sufficiently large following, if the timing and subject matter are right, and if the publisher does an unusually effective job of publicity and promotion, it is entirely possible for a book that receives a bad press to sell well or even become a best seller.

The above does not, incidentally, apply to children's books. Schools and libraries are the largest buyers of these titles, and their purchases are greatly influenced by reviews found in specialized magazines such as *School Library Journal, Kirkus Reviews, ALA Booklist, The Horn Book,* and the *Bulletin of the Center for Children's Books.* The larger school and public library systems have their own committees that select the books for purchase—thus, in effect, having their own reviewers, whose advice is closely followed. The publicity and promotion departments of a publishing house which publishes children's books must, of course, keep in contact with these large local school and library sys-

Important periodicals in the reviewing of children's books

tems and send them free review copies of each book as they do to the nationwide review media.

Beyond reviews for adult books—and considered even more effective—is work that will lead to bringing news of the book, or of the author, to those readers who are not necessarily influenced by book reviews. This off-the-book-page publicity generally calls for an author's willingness to participate personally in the promotion of a book. It also calls for careful, intelligent judgment on the part of the publicity director as to whether or not such treatment is feasible—it certainly wouldn't be for most novels, for example—and whether or not the author possesses an attractive "public" personality. Writers write, and there is no reason to believe that a brilliant author will necessarily have the kind of personality that projects effectively in public appearances of any kind. Many authors are shy and are unable to help in publicizing their books. Others feel (mistakenly, because a purpose of writing a book is having it read by as many people as possible) that cooperating in the publicity for their book is somehow beneath them. For the most part, however, authors are more than willing—actually, most eager—to help in any way possible.

One medium for off-the-book-page publicity is the printed word—a newspaper or a magazine. If an author reveals timely, newsworthy, or even sensational information in his or her book, it may be worthy of a news or feature story or possibly an interview with the author, in a section of the newspaper or magazine other

The cover from Alexandra Wallner's book 'Munch'

I won't be a fat old husband,
I can't stand a piggy wife,
Would you please, so very kindly,
Pass the butter, jam and knife?

Mary, Mary, bellyache,
Thinks that ice cream's really great,
Eats a gallon, then one more,
Eats every flavor in the store.

She dishes out poetry
that you can 'Munch' to

By Jill Gerston
Inquirer Staff Writer

Alexandra Wallner loves to munch — pretzels, sesame sticks, fudge brownies and just about any yummy that happens to be in her well-stocked cupboard.

She also loves to write poetry and draw whimsical little pen and ink sketches. So what could be more natural for her than to write an illustrated volume of verse appropriately titled "Munch?"

"The idea came about so easily — I just thought of everyday situations involving myself, my family and my friends," said Mrs. Wallner, 29, a plump, size 16 brunette who lives in Brooklyn Heights, N. Y. with her illustrator husband, John.

Her friends and relatives bounce through the 30-page book in the guise of fashionably dressed pigs, hippos and elephants who gather at parties and picnics to devour triple-decker sandwiches, "ginger marshmello" ice cream cones and innumerable boxes of chocolate butter creams.

Among the munchers is "Mary, Mary Bellyache," an ice-cream slurping hippo who hangs out in Ed's ice cream store and is, according to the author, a parody of an aunt who is addicted to Baskin-Robbins.

The T-shirt clad elephant who is eating his jam-splattered way to Peanut Butter Heaven was inspired by Mrs. Wallner's husband, who felt that "Munch" would be incomplete without the "ultimate peanut butter orgy."

Mrs. Wallner doesn't hesitate to poke fun at herself and her spouse, each of whom, she said, has gained "at least" 25 pounds since their marriage 4½ years ago. They are portrayed in the book as well-to-do husband and wife piggies who enjoy a leisurely snack of grape jam and bread. Accompanying the picture is the poem:

"I won't be a fat old husband,
I can't stand a piggy wife,
Would you please, so very kindly,
Pass me the butter, jam and knife?"

Mrs. Wallner's favorite character, however, is a fictional "Russian Czarina," whom she dreamed up to illustrate the fanciful jingle:

"There once was a Russian Czarina,
Who ate nothing but milk and farina.
She grew big and fat,
Was ashamed of all that,
So she yachted her way to Argentina."

Mrs. Wallner, an ebullient former magazine illustrator whose nickname is Lexi and whose nemesis is Italian food and French pastry, said that "Munch" does not moralize or depict fatties in a derogatory manner. Instead, the author went on, the book "celebrates food and the joy of eating."

Right now, Mrs. Wallner said she's working on several children's stories, none of which contains any mention of food.

What about doing a book for skinny-minnies, say something along the lines of sparrows and storks nibbling on carrot sticks and lettuce leaves?

"No way," laughed the food-loving author. "I just don't have an affinity for drawing straight lines. I like big, rounded shapes. Who ever heard of a chubby stork?

Philadelphia Inquirer
PHILADELPHIA, PA.
D. 463,503 SUN. 867,810

FEB 16 1976

Off-the-book-page newspaper publicity

than the space reserved for books. A fashion editor might be interested in a book on fashion, just as a political editor would interest himself in a book on politics, a food editor in a cookbook, a financial editor in a book on the stock market. These interests could lead to articles that would be read even by those people (and there are far too many of them) who read but a few books a year.

There is little more that a publicity department can do with the printed word: through newspaper or magazine pieces a book can become a topic of conversation (controversy is helpful), or the author can become a "personality." These are, of course, highly effective means of publicizing a book, but there are other ways in which a publicity director will try to make a book known to the public. A few examples will suffice.

Though it is less common today than it was in the past, publishers sometimes give publication parties. They are often held in glamorous locations or unusual ones such as boats, railroad cars, or even exotic places that are relevant to the theme of the book. These parties can be costly, but they can serve to call attention to a given book, or even be occasions for the members of a publishing house to get to know members of the review media.

In addition, there are sometimes autographing parties held in bookstores, though these seem to be of little value, since most people don't really care for an autographed book unless the author is already famous. The

```
                          INSANITY INSIDE OUT by Ken Donaldson
June 21    New York    10:00 am          NBC-Radio. News information feature.
                                         30 Rockefeller Plaza -- room 832.
                                         Barry Cornet, contact. CI7-8300.

                       Noon              WRVR-Radio. Interview with Bob Siegel.
                                         120 St. 6 Claremont Avenue. 678-6855.

                       6:17 pm           WSB-Radio (Atlanta). Phone interview
                                         with Gordon Van Mol. He will call you
                                         at Ruth Aley's number.

                       7:20 pm           KDKA-Radio (Pittsburgh). Newsmakers.
                                         Phone interview. They will call you
June 22    FLY TO MIAMI                  at Ruth Aley's number.

TRANSPORTATION: Eastern Flight #29 leaves LaGuardia at 6:00 pm; arrives at Miami
                at 8:44 pm

ACCOMODATIONS:  Four Ambassadors Hotel

June 23    Miami       8:30 am           WPLG-TV. AM Miami. 3900 Biscayne Blvd.
                                         Frank Lynn, contact. 305-573-7111.

                       1:00 pm           MIAMI HERALD interview. Herald Plaza --
                                         5th floor. Caroline Hecht, contact.
                                         305-350-2688.
```

A portion of author Kenneth Donaldson's media schedule

appearance of an unknown author at a poorly attended autographing party in his or her honor could be most embarrassing for author and publisher alike. Some institutions, however, hold book fairs at which several authors appear, and these fairs can be useful: they may result in few copies sold at the time, but they help to spread the word of the book's publication. Some publishers, too, help to arrange lecture tours for an author, if the author is articulate and personable, and these too can greatly stimulate interest in a book.

The list of possibilities for publicity is almost endless, but of all means of creating interest in a book, the most effective in recent years has been the television appearance. Television, of course, reaches an enormous audience, many of whom are not regular book readers, but who will occasionally purchase a book if persuaded to do so. And television, as has been demonstrated, can be most persuasive. There are, unfortunately, very few programs devoted to books alone, but an appearance by an interesting author on one or many "talk" shows can result in the sale of many copies of his or her book.

However, as effective as television (and, to a lesser extent, radio) appearances are, a wise publicity director will know that the large majority of authors are not suitable for use on these media for a number of reasons. One reason is that most authors do not have the sense of showmanship necessary for television appearances. Next, unfortunately, television programs don't want most authors as guests. It is useless even to try to place an unknown author (a first novelist, for example, would not even be considered except in very rare cases) on a television program unless the book is of unusually wide interest and is, preferably, a controversial one. Even a well-known literary figure, unless he or she is especially colorful, will find it impossible to compete for television time with the author of a book who is best known in another field such as show business or sports, psychology or cooking.

Undoubtedly, television can do a great deal to influence the sales of a book–repeated appearances are best–but undoubtedly, too, it can be used by a very small number of authors in the promotion of their books.

Effective, as well, is a tour for the author to a few or

several cities throughout the country, making use of each stop for local newspaper interviews, television and radio appearances, and meetings with local reviewers and booksellers. However, just as in the case of television programs, these tours must be limited to special authors, since once again there would be little interest in appearances by or interviews with relatively unknown authors. In addition, the costs of such tours can be high in both time and money since the author is normally accompanied by a member of the publicity department or, in some cases, a local representative—either the publisher's salesman, or someone hired especially for the job.

The most costly way of promoting a book—by advertising it—has been left for last, since many publishers believe it is far less effective than do their authors. In fact, many publishers say that they advertise more to please their authors than to sell books.

Initial advertising in trade journals such as *Publishers Weekly* or *Library Journal* is considered worthwhile as a form of announcement to the librarian and bookseller. This advertising, relatively inexpensive, also demonstrates a confidence in a book. Beyond that, advertising is very costly, and the budget for most books does not leave room for more than one—or maybe two—token ads in major newspapers. Strangely, it is widely believed that advertising is most usefully employed *after* a book has started to sell (it can turn a good seller into a best seller), and very little money is budgeted for the adver-

Books for children and teenagers from Crown

FALL 1976

Little Fox Goes to the End of the World

By ANN TOMPERT. Illustrated in four colors by JOHN WALLNER. When Little Fox grows tired of playing near the mouth of her den, she embarks on a daring journey of the imagination, encouraged by her mother's playfulness. A Junior Literary Guild Selection. Ages 4-7. August. *RLB (52600X) $6.95

Two is Company

By JUDY DELTON. Illustrated in three colors by GIULIO MAESTRO. In this story suited for beginning readers, Bear and Duck are two good friends until Chipmunk moves into the neighborhood. Duck befriends Chipmunk, and Bear becomes jealous, but an unexpected act of friendship leads to a change of heart. Ages 5-8. August. *RLB (526018) $4.95

The Rats Who Lived in the Delicatessen

Written and illustrated in four colors by HAROLD BERSON. Stan's life was paradise inside a delicatessen, even after Morris and his large family moved in. But when they were joined by other hungry rats, a fight broke out that brought another animal running — and that animal was the only one who remained. Ages 4-7. August. *RLB (526042) $5.95

The Bear & the Fly

Illustrated in three colors by PAULA WINTER. In this wordless picture book, the chaos caused by an elusive fly turns the bears' family dinner into a disaster. Ages 3-5. July. *RLB (526050) $4.95

Mr. Tamarin's Trees

By KATHRYN ERNST. Illustrated in four colors by DIANE DE GROAT. When Mr. Tamarin cuts down the trees on his property to stop the leaves from falling, his wife assures him that he will regret it someday. Mr. Tamarin tells her, "Never," but time and the passing of seasons change his mind. Ages 4-7. July. *RLB (526158) $5.95

Toliver's Secret

By ESTHER WOOD BRADY. Illustrated by RICHARD CUFFARI. Ten-year-old Ellen Toliver proves she has courage, intelligence and imagination when she becomes part of a chain of couriers who will carry an important message to General Washington. An adventure novel that richly details life in America during the Revolution. Ages 8-10. September. (526212) $6.95

Books: From Writer to Reader

By HOWARD GREENFELD. The numerous people involved in publishing are introduced and their various responsibilities are discussed in this comprehensive and lucid account of how books are created. Illustrated throughout in four colors and black-and-white. A Junior Literary Guild Selection. All ages. October. (526204) $8.95

*Reinforced Library Binding
Please add our prefix, 0-517-,
to all code numbers to get full ISBN's.
Illustration by John Wallner from
Little Fox Goes to the End of the World.
CROWN PUBLISHERS, INC.
One Park Ave., New York, N.Y. 10016

Publisher's list ad for children's books

tising of all but a limited number of what seem to be mass-appeal books. A book will be widely advertised if there are early indications of extra monies that the book will earn—such as a good paperback sale or a movie sale. However, the fact is that little money is spent on advertising most books, and the reasons for this have proved to be valid.

Advertising is one way of persuading people to buy a book, but as we have seen, there are other—and usually less expensive—ways available which can be equally or more effective. The essential element is an imaginative publicity department, whose job in its way can be as creative as that of any other individual or group taking part in the long process of publishing a book.

Afterword

These chapters have dealt with the creation of books, the making of books, and the publishing—making public—of books. A great deal has been written about editing, designing, printing, binding, bookselling, publicizing, but it is important not to lose sight of the ultimate reason for all of these procedures—the books themselves, and the ideas and pleasures that they bring to the reader.

As we have seen, books don't just happen: a great amount of talent, skill, and hard work is involved each step of the way. There are techniques and methods and changing technologies, yet no book could exist without the miracle that lies behind it—the human mind.

Glossary

aa (author's alterations) Corrections made in galleys by the author.

acetate A sheet of clear plastic film taped over artwork as an overlay.

acknowledgment Part of a book, generally in the front matter, acknowledging thanks or credit to those who helped with the book.

ad card Part of a book, generally in the front matter, listing other books by the same author, also called card page.

advance Payment by the publisher to the author before the book is published, to be deducted from future earnings.

appendix Additional useful information related to but not part of the main text of a book, generally found in the back matter.

artwork The assembled parts of a mechanical to be used as camera copy.

ascender That part of a lower-case letter which extends above the main body of that letter, as in "d" or "b."

back matter All material that follows the main body of the text, such as appendix, bibliography, glossary, index.

bibliography A list of source materials and supplementary reading relevant to the book, usually a part of the back matter.

binding die An engraving used to impress letters or a design on the binding of a book.

bleed An illustration which extends to the very edge of the trimmed page.

blueprints (blues) A photoprint made from the assembled films used in making offset plates. Blues serve as final proofs.

blurb A description of the book printed on the flaps or the back of the jacket.

boldface A type used for emphasis, thicker than the text type with which it is used.

BOM proofs Proofs, especially cut and bound for easier reading, which are submitted to book clubs or are used for publicity purposes.

bulk The thickness of paper, or sometimes the thickness of a book.

calender To pass paper between cylinders under pressure. The way in which this is done determines the smoothness and glossiness of the surface of the paper.

camera copy Material to be photographed for platemaking.

camera-separated artwork Artwork which is to be separated into different colors for printing by use of a camera.

caption Identification of an illustration, usually printed under that illustration.

case In printing, a compartmented tray in which type is kept; in binding, the covers of a hardbound book.

casting The procedure in which molten metal is forced against a mold, then cooled and hardened to produce type or lines of type.

castoff An estimate of the number of pages a book will be when it is set in type.

chapter heads The numbers of the chapters.

chapter opening The first page of a chapter.

chapter title The title of a chapter.

character Each letter, numeral, symbol, and punctuation mark of a font.

character count The number of letters, symbols, numerals, punctuation marks, and spaces that a manuscript contains.

cold type Type set by direct impression without the use of metal.

color separation The process of separating full color into the primary printing colors by means of photography with color filters.

color swatches Specimens or samples which indicate the precise color to be used in printing.

contents A list of the entire contents of a book, generally part of the front matter.

copy Any material to be composed or photographed for printing.

copyright The exclusive right, given by law for a number of years, to make and sell a work of literature, music, or art. In the case of a book (which cannot be copyrighted unless printed and sold), a notice to this effect must be printed either on the title page or on the reverse of the title page.

dedication An inscription, generally part of the front matter, dedicating a book to a person, persons, or a cause.

descender That part of a lower-case letter which extends below the main body of that letter, as in "p" or "y."

display type Letters set larger than the text, to draw attention.

double-spread Two facing pages, designed as a single unit.

dummy Pages which show the size, shape, and general appearance of a book, often including a rough layout with the position of text and illustrations.

endpapers Folded paper, sturdier than that used for the text and often colored or decorated, pasted to the insides of the front and back covers of a book for binding.

estimate A calculation of the cost of a book, or the number of pages it will contain.

extract Special text matter set off typographically or by the use of indentation from the main body of the text.

f & g's Printed sheets, folded and gathered in proper sequence, preliminary to binding.

flat Assemblage of films, stripped on goldenrod paper in their proper arrangement, for use in making offset plates.

flat sheets Printed sheets before they have been folded for binding.

flush A line of type, set to line up at right or left.

folio A page number.

font The complete assortment of type, of one face and size.

footnote Supplementary notation at the bottom of a page which refers to material on that page.

foreword An introductory statement, by the author or another person. Part of the front matter.

fountain, ink The device in a printing press which stores ink and then supplies it to rollers.

four-color presses Printing presses that can apply four different colors simultaneously.

frontispiece An illustration facing the title page of a book.

front matter All material which precedes the main text of a book.

full measure The full width of a line of type, flush with both margins.

galley A shallow metal drawer or tray in which type and cuts are kept after setting.

galley proofs (galleys) The first proofs pulled, before the type has been divided into pages.

gathering Bringing together the signatures of a book for binding.

glossary A list of special terms used in a book, with their definitions.

goldenrod A specially treated orange yellow paper, on which films are positioned for the making of offset plates.

gravure An intaglio method of printing; the printing areas which retain the ink on the plate are depressed.

half title The title of the book set in smaller letters than on the title page and usually found on the first page of the book.

hot type Type set by cast metal by hand or by machine (Linotype or Monotype).

imposition The arrangement of pages in a press form, so that they will be in proper sequence when folded for binding.

impression cylinder The cylinder that presses the pages against the inked surfaces for printing.

indentation The setting of a line of type to less than the full width of the page.

index A list of proper nouns, terms, and sometimes concepts used in the text, with their corresponding page numbers, which is part of the back matter of a book.

inside margin The distance from the inner edge of the page to the beginning of the type area.

Intertype A typesetting machine which casts each line as a solid line of type; it is similar to linotype.

introduction A formal statement of the scope and purpose of the book, sometimes part of the front matter and sometimes part of the text itself.

italics Slanted letters, used in the text for emphasis.

justify To space out lines to the correct uniform width.

key plate In color printing, the plate (usually black) containing the outline which is used as a guide for the other colors.

layout The drawing or sketch of all the elements on a page in proper position.

leading The space between lines of type.

line art Copy that contains only solid blacks and whites and thus can be reproduced without gradation in tone.

Linofilm A method of phototypesetting with the use of perforated tape.

Linotype A typesetting machine which casts each line as a solid line of type.

lower case Uncapitalized letters of the alphabet.

Ludlow A typesetting machine used largely for setting display type.

magazine The part of the composing machine in which the matrices of the letters are stored.

makeup Arrangement of all elements—type and illustration—into page form.

margin The white space on all four sides of the printed area of a page.

matrix A mold in which typefaces are cast.

Monotype A typesetting machine which casts each character separately, as with hand-set type.

mechanical Camera-ready pasteup of all elements on one piece of artboard for use in offset platemaking.

negative A transparent photographic film on which light values and image are reversed (the black shows as white, left is right, etc.).

offset (blanket) cylinder A cylinder onto which a rubber blanket is attached and which transfers the image from the plate to the paper in offset printing.

opaquing Painting out on a negative the areas that are not wanted on a plate.

page proofs (pages) Impression of the type after division into page form.

part title The title or number of a major part of a book, generally printed on a separate page preceding that part.

perfect binding A method of binding, without stitching or sewing, in which the signatures are held together by an adhesive.

photostats An economically reproduced photograph made with the use of special equipment, often used for layouts and dummies.

pica A measurement, which equals twelve points or approximately one-sixth of an inch, used by printers to measure lines.

positive A print made from a negative, showing the original light values and images.

plant cost Nonrecurring expenses in the manufacture of a book, such as composition and plates.

point The basic unit of type measurement; there are approximately 72 points to an inch.

printer's error (pe) An error made by the compositor.

progressive proofs (progs) Proofs used in color process printing which show each color alone and then in combination with other colors.

proofs Trial impressions of composed type or illustrations, taken to correct errors and make changes.

registering Precisely superimposing in correct relationship the various colors in color printing.

register marks Crosses or other devices used as a guide to registering.

reproduction proofs (repros) Proofs on specially coated paper to be used as camera copy for offset platemaking.

roman The ordinary upright type style, as opposed to slanted italics.

rough layout A preliminary sketch of a layout meant for general effect and not detail.

royalty The author's percentage of the proceeds from the sales of a book, generally based on the retail price.

running heads The book, part, or chapter title repeated at the top of each page of a book.

serif A short line extending from the main stroke of a letter in some typefaces.

signature A folded, printed sheet of a book, usually sixteen or thirty-two pages.

sinkage The distance from the top of the page to the highest element on a type page.

small caps Capital letters that are smaller in size than regular capitals.

Smyth sewing A method of binding by means of threads which are passed through each signature and locked at the back.

specifications, type The complete instructions for composition.

spine The part of the binding that connects the two covers.

staining Coloring the edges of a book.

text type The type used for the main body of the text as opposed to the headings.

title page The part of the front matter that contains the title of the book, the name of the author, and the name of the publisher.

trim size The size of the pages after the paper has been trimmed.

typeface Any design of type, including the full range of characters (letters, numbers, and punctuation marks) in every size.

typescript Typewritten copy.

type size The size of type designated by points which measure the distance from the top of the highest character in a font to the bottom of the lowest.

upper case Capital letters.

value The degree of lightness or darkness of a tone or color.

Bibliography

Bliven, Bruce, Jr. *Book Traveller.* New York: Dodd, Mead & Company, 1975.

Grannis, Chandler B. (ed.). *What Happens in Book Publishing.* New York: Columbia University Press, 1957.

Gross, Gerald (ed.). *Editors on Editing.* New York: Grosset & Dunlap, Inc., 1962.
Publishers on Publishing. New York: Grosset & Dunlap, Inc., 1961.

International Paper Company. *Pocket Pal*, 11th ed. New York: 1974.

Kingman, Lee (ed.). *Newbery and Caldecott Medal Books: 1956–1965.* Boston: The Horn Book, 1965.

Lee, Marshall. *Bookmaking.* New York: R. R. Bowker Company, 1965.

Melcher, Daniel, and Larrick, Nancy. *Printing and Promotion Handbook.* New York: McGraw-Hill, Inc., 1956.

Steinberg, S. H. *Five Hundred Years of Printing,* 3rd ed. Baltimore: Penguin Books Inc., 1974.

Strauss, Victor. *The Printing Industry.* Washington, D.C.:
    Printing Industries of America, 1967.

University of Chicago. *A Manual of Style,* 12th ed. Chicago:
    University of Chicago Press, 1969.

Williamson, Hugh. *Methods of Book Design.* New York:
    Oxford University Press, Inc., 1956.

Index